SZ

MILLER'S
COLLECTING
KITCHENWARE

MILLER'S
COLLECTING
KITCHENWARE

CHRISTINA BISHOP

MILLER'S

Miller's Collecting Kitchenware
Christina Bishop

First published in Great Britain in 1995
by Miller's, an imprint of Reed Books Limited
Michelin House, 81 Fulham Road
London SW3 6RB
and Auckland, Melbourne, Singapore and Toronto

Miller's is a registered trademark of Reed International
Books Limited
© 1995 Reed International Books Limited,
Reprinted 1996

Executive Editor Alison Starling
Executive Art Editor Vivienne Brar
Editor Francesca Collin
Designer Maggie Town at Town Group Consultancy
Production Heather O'Connell
Index Hilary Bird

Front jacket photograph by Hugh Johnson
Special photography by Martin Norris, with additional
photography by James Merrell (p.2, p.12, p.32, p.42,
p.50, p.78, p.92, p.110 and p.124)

Produced by Mandarin Offset
Printed and bound in Hong Kong

A CIP catalogue for this book is available from the
British Library.

ISBN 1 85732 565 6

Set in M Baskerville and Univers Condensed.

Contents

INTRODUCTION

There is something truly special about cooking and baking with items that have been used by previous generations of women and in *Miller's Collecting Kitchenware* I hope to lead you through the kitchen door and introduce you to the pleasures of collecting our domestic heritage.

This book concentrates on items produced from the 1890s to the 1950s, arguably the most interesting period in the development of kitchenware. The 19th century saw the introduction of many designs that were to remain unchanged until today, such as the balloon whisk and the pastry crimper. In the 20th century, mass production led to the development of kitchenware as a huge international industry, with British makers such as Tala and Nutbrown leading the field.

Although many designs have not altered since the 19th century, different materials have come in and out of fashion. For instance, in the 19th century, cast iron was commonly used for pots and pans, along with steel. By the early 20th century, aluminium, lighter and more versatile, was favoured, especially in North America. From the 1920s onwards, stainless steel became the most popular metal for making cutlery. By the mid-20th century, plastic began to dominate the kitchenware industry: cheap and durable, it proved a resounding success and is still widely used today.

One of the greatest joys of collecting kitchenware is in using it. I take great pleasure in cooking with items that have been called into service over many years and in imagining who worked with them before me. Remember though that older items will need more looking after than new ones, so take extra care with washing and drying up. Store items safely in a dry place to prevent them from becoming rusty.

Kitchenware offers enormous scope to collectors, who can choose from favourite mainstream areas, such as storage jars or pie funnels, to more obscure subjects, such as whisks, wooden spoons or griddles. Other collectors prefer to concentrate on a specific type of material, such as wirework or enamel.

Whatever you choose, all these implements and utensils are still easy to find today, often for only a few pounds, and much enjoyment can be had from tracking them down in car boot sales, markets or even junk shops.

The familiarity of many pieces of kitchenware today often belies their unusual history. For instance, the Doulton 'improved' bread pan of the 19th century was produced by a company that also made bathroom fittings and drainage pipes; and, until the 1920s, food safes were always built off the ground to keep hungry mice and rats away.

It is also interesting to observe how kitchenware has adapted to changing tastes in food. Domestic coffee grinders were first used in the 18th century, when it became fashionable to drink coffee at home rather than in coffee houses. In the 19th century great attention was given to the presentation of food, hence the enormous variety of moulds from this period, used to make a savoury or sweet jelly, blancmange or mousse as an impressive centrepiece. In the 20th century tastes changed again. Tea parties became popular with the middle and upper classes in Britain, leading to a wide array of useful gadgets for making dainty cakes and sandwiches, such as egg slicers, cake baking tins and icing kits. Similarly, it is intriguing to see how kitchenware differs from country to country. Kitchenware is an enormous and diverse area and over 300 items have been specially photographed for this book, and each item

has been given an individual price guide. Price guides are notoriously difficult to compile as there are so many different sources for kitchenware and prices reflect this diversity. Geographical location, availability of particular items and the overheads of the dealer all play their part.

Antiques shops, auction houses, car boot sales and specialist kitchenware dealers all have their own price ranges and you should use the prices featured in *Miller's Collecting Kitchenware* only as a guide. Remember, the price guides are for what you should expect to pay for items featured, not what you could sell them for to an antiques shop or a dealer.

Perhaps the best source of kitchenware is direct from your mother, grandmother or aunt, who can explain first-hand how a particular item was used in her kitchen. Ask questions and listen; it is a fascinating journey and one that should bring you much pleasure and enjoyment.

Christina Bishop

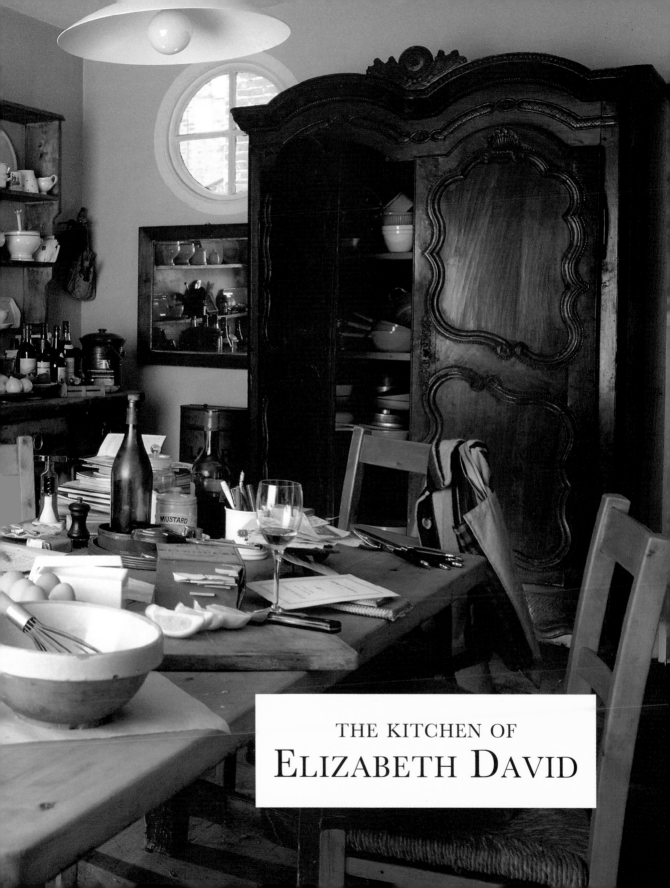

THE KITCHEN OF
ELIZABETH DAVID

Elizabeth David (1913–1992) is possibly the most important cook to have lived this century. Often credited with single-handedly changing the British attitude to food and eating. A prolific cookery writer, she published her first book, *A Book of Mediterranean Food*, published in 1950, introduced deprived readers to the delights of French and Italian cooking. This was

Previous page One of Elizabeth David's two kitchens in her Chelsea house, designed for her by her nephew, Johnny Grey. *Below* A photograph of Elizabeth David in the 1950s, along with her collection of cookery books.

followed by more best-sellers, such as *French Country Cooking* (1951), *Summer Cooking* (1955), *French Provincial Cooking* (1960), *English Bread and Yeast* (1977), and *An Omelette and a Glass of Wine* (1984).

David wrote all these books from her house in Chelsea, London, where she lived from 1949 until her death in 1992, at the age of 78. The contents of house, particularly the two kitchens – one for winter, the other for summer – reflect David's whole approach to cooking. Designed in a simple but effective way by David's nephew, Johnny Grey, an established kitchen designer, they were not 'fitted' as was fashionable at the time, but comprised a selection of utilitarian furniture, such as plain wooden cupboards, tables, dressers, large stone sinks and straightforward cookers, and each was furnished with an extensive selection of traditional kitchen utensils and equipment.

David did not use any modern machines, preferring traditional equipment. 'My cooking is mostly on a small scale and of the kind for intimate friends, so I'm happy enough with an ordinary four-burner gas stove,' she once wrote.

'It's probably best for cookery writers to use the same kind of domestic equipment as the majority of their readers. It doesn't do to get too far away from the problems of everyday household cooking or take the easy way out with expensive gadgetry.'

David is known to have rarely thrown anything away. As a result, her collection of kitchenware was enormous. To her, these items in themselves provided enough decoration to a room, and she once said that if the food and cooking pots did not provide enough visual interest in a kitchen then there was something wrong.

Following her death, the contents of David's kitchens were sold by Phillips the auctioneers in London in 1994, raising a staggering total of over £49,000 on 176 lots.

In the full glare of the media, cooks and kitchenware enthusiasts from around the world gathered in London for the chance to buy an item from one of the world's most famous cooks. Kitchen equipment, such as pots, pans, wooden spoons and other utensils were quickly sold to this enthusiastic audience, often for far more than their original auction estimates.

A large part of the sale consisted of books and ephemera, including a collection of trade cards, and two albums containing cards and cuttings. David was a compulsive note-taker and many of her cookery books were personally annotated with comments about each recipe.

The enormous success of the auction played a major part in raising the status of kitchenware, reflecting its established popularity and introducing it to a wider international audience.

Above A jug full of wooden spoons and forks, belonging to Elizabeth David, which sold for an amazing £400 at Phillips' auction in London in February 1994.

David's total rejection of the modern fashion for fitted kitchens and up-to-date gadgets and equipment is clearly revealed in her writing: 'Devote all the time and resources at your disposal to the building of a fine kitchen. It will be, as it should be, the most comforting and comfortable room in the house.

What it amounts to is that for me the perfect kitchen would really be more like a painter's studio and should be furnished with cooking equipment than anything conventionally accepted as a kitchen.'

STORAGE

Traditionally, food has been stored in containers made from the most easily available local materials, such as wood, pottery and cloth. From the 19th century onwards, storage jars were mass-produced by manufacturers. Sets of different-sized jars for herbs, spices and other ingredients were made, often in attractive decorative designs, and enamelled metal jars were common too. These could be bought plain from a hardware store and the local shopkeeper would stencil on the desired name, such as 'Flour' or 'Tea' for a small charge. Enamel bread bins and flour bins were particularly popular in Britain and, remarkably, designs have not altered greatly today.

Food safes – wooden cupboards used for storing food – were found in most homes before the introduction of refrigerators in the mid-20th century, although wealthier houses had cool stone-flagged walk-in larders, where dry ingredients, fresh fruit and vegetables could be stored alongside meat, game and fish.

Other types of storage included attractive wirework baskets and containers used for carrying items such as fish, bottles or vegetables and for storing eggs or fruit. They were often beautifully made by hand from twisted wire. Beware of lesser-quality modern reproductions made today!

▼ A 1950s wooden tea box with a sliding lid.

TEA, COFFEE & SUGAR

Although tea is now the world's best-loved drink, its chequered history had a great impact on its popularity. First introduced into Europe and America in the 17th century, when the age of exploration opened up new trade links with the West Indies and China, tea was initially a luxury product. It was afforded only by the very wealthy, who stored their tea leaves in locked wooden tea caddies to stop the servants from stealing it!

By the mid-19th century, other tea-producing countries had started to export tea too. Now that it was affordable, people bought larger amounts and needed storage containers and tea caddies. It was important to keep tea dry and away from the light.

From the mid-1850s onwards, coffee was more commonly brewed at home and needed storage too. Tins, japanned bins, wooden barrels and sacks were used in both Europe and North America at this time. Pottery, enamel and aluminium were adopted in Europe after 1900.

◄ This early 1960s hand-painted jar by the English potter, Toni Raymond, has a distinctive mark on the base, depicting a goose in flight. The wooden lid is attached by a rubber seal for air-tight freshness. Storage jars became less imaginative in design from the mid-1960s onwards. By the 1980s, reproductions of early designs were popular, but are not collectable.

£10–15

▲ This set of 1920s French aluminium storage jars for sugar, coffee and chicory reflects how tastes differ throughout the world. Chicory is a very popular drink in France, but is rarely found elsewhere. The roots of the plant are roasted and dried and used either as a coffee substitute or mixed with coffee to make it last longer. There was a fashion for chicory in Britain in the 1930s, but it would seem that it was short-lived, as no containers for chicory are known ever to have been made.

£35–40

▲ Graduating storage sets, such as this French pottery set, are attractive but impractical: the flour pot can hold approximately only ½lb (200g) of flour! Art Deco in style, this set from the 1930s is high in value, as this period is so popular. Similar graduating sets were made in the 1950s, in larger sizes.

£65–85

▼ Storage containers were produced for other drinks, such as cocoa and chocolate powder, from the mid-19th century onwards. Storage tins for cocoa are particularly rare, especially this enamel one from the 1930s. Enamel containers do not devalue if chipped, but the interior must be in perfect condition if it is to be used.

£15–20

▼ First imported to Europe and America in the 18th century, from the West Indies, sugar came to replace honey as a drink sweetener, as well as an important cooking ingredient, particularly in cities. This painted tin with gilt lettering was made in Britain between 1900 and the 1920s and it is rare to see the lettering still intact.

£10–15

▲ This type of attractive gilt-coloured tin coffee canister was made between the 1880s and the 1930s. The material is still in remarkably good condition – tin damages very easily and the insides of tin containers need to be rust-free if they are going to be re-used for storage. Always check tinware carefully.

£15–20

PRESERVES & COOKING INGREDIENTS

Storage jars for preserves and cooking ingredients have not greatly changed since they were first commercially produced in the mid-19th century. Although large families would need to store ingredients in huge quantities, most pantries or larders could accommodate only medium-sized jars, roughly the same size as jam jars produced today. The range of ingredients required has not altered greatly either, with flour, rice and dried fruit the most commonly found, although products such as tapioca and sago are less widely used today. Storage tins for more unusual products are the most sought after.

Until World War II, containers were often bought plain from local hardware shops and labels for particular ingredients were either added at home or stencilled on at the shop for a small fee. Today, jars with homemade painted lettering are the least valuable. Slightly more collectable are plain jars, while jars with the original shop-made labels command the highest prices.

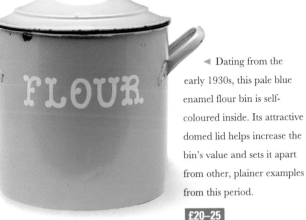

◀ Dating from the early 1930s, this pale blue enamel flour bin is self-coloured inside. Its attractive domed lid helps increase the bin's value and sets it apart from other, plainer examples from this period.

£20–25

▼ Kilner jars were first launched to the British public in 1861 at the National Exhibition – a showcase for contemporary designers. Used mainly for preserving fruit, the Kilner jar's main feature was a secure screw-top lid with a rubber ring seal to ensure extra freshness. This one is an 'improved' Kilner jar, introduced in the late 1940s; the improvement lay in the jar's ability to keep items fresher for longer.

Under £5 each

▼ The brown lettering on this flour bin from the mid-1920s is very rare and adds considerably to its value. The bin is also unusually large – it is capable of holding over 28lb (12.6kg) of flour and it was probably made specially for use in schools and institutions.

£28–34

DETECTING FLOUR MITES

This advice for detecting flour mites was first given in a guide written for housekeepers, hotels and restaurants and was published in the 1930s:

'If flour develops a sour smell, it is probable that it has been contaminated by flour mites and should be thrown away immediately. These microscopic creatures often find their way into the flour before leaving the mills or factories and can ruin a whole bag. To check for mites, take a spoonful and press between two flat glass surfaces. Separate the glass, leaving a thin layer of flour. If mites are present, bumps will occur, indicating the mites are moving to the surface for air.'

◄ Metal flour bins were first used in the 19th century. Mid-Victorian ones were made of enamelled iron, which made them very heavy. Later versions, such as this one with raised lettering and trim, is from the late 1930s and holds about 3lb (1.35kg) of flour.

£15–18

► Breadcrumbs are often used as a thickener for sauces, but it is unusual to see a storage container for them, as they need to be stale and crisp and a jar would keep them fresh and moist. Although this stone china jar was made c.1900, the lettering was probably added later. Green lettering is typical of this period, but was also popular in the 1930s.

£14–18

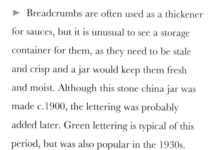

◄ Produced in large numbers and sometimes painted, early English wooden flour barrels, such as this 19th-century example, were also used to store butter. By the 20th century, wooden barrels had been replaced by more durable and hygienic metal and pottery containers.

£65–85

17

► These three pottery jars are all slightly different. The one on the left was made for James Keiller & Sons of Scotland, famous makers of marmalade. Established in 1797, they used this type of jar from 1873 until the late 1950s and the only way to distinguish later ones is by checking the mark under the crest. This one has a 'Y', which dates it from pre-1945; jars made from 1945 onwards have an 'L'. The large jar in the centre can hold up to 2lb (900g) of Robertson's mincemeat. The jar on the right for Flett & Co.'s apple and plum jam (a Scottish grocers) and the Robertson's jar still have their original labels, which adds to their appeal.

£5–15 each

▼ Pottery dried fruit containers, such as this hand-painted example, were made in Austria from the late 1950s to the early 1960s for the export market. Sweden produced containers in similar designs during this period too, and it is likely that Sweden conceived the idea first, as the designs are more typically Scandinavian than Austrian. In both countries, sets could be built up to include jars for other ingredients, such as rice, sugar and flour.

£15–18

ROBERTSON'S

One of Britain's most famous manufacturers of preserves and jams, Robertson's were set up by James Robertson, whose first company was a grocery shop in Scotland in the 1860s. His move into manufacturing came about after he had been persuaded to buy a barrel of bitter oranges by a local salesman. Sales were slow and so his wife, Marion, offered to use them to make marmalade. The marmalade proved so popular that before long the Robertsons had to expand their business and opened a factory in the 1890s, which came to be known as the 'Golden Shred Works'.

The famous Golly trademark was first introduced in 1910, quickly becoming such a popular symbol that enamel Golly brooches were introduced in 1928 which could be sent for in return for a number of vouchers.

This scheme was halted by Robertson's in 1939 on the eve of World War II, as the metal was needed for the war effort, but relaunched in 1945 with ten different Golly brooches to collect. Robertson's still run the scheme today, although there is a small charge for the Golly brooches, which are now made of painted metal.

► These 1890s stoneware storage jars make an attractive set, particularly with the ribbon design labels. They were made from the 1880s to the 1920s and the only way to date them is by checking the colour carefully in good light – the buff colour became lighter over the years. Keep an eye out for ¼lb (100g) spice jars, as these are the rarest, and choose jars with lids.

£15–35 each

◄ Large sets of storage jars, such as this Edwardian set, are particularly sought after, especially if they include storage containers for more unusual ingredients, such as tapioca and barley (see also the cake tin on p.26). It is worth noting that, although they may look attractive, these enamelled containers are not very practical as their lids are not airtight. It is less expensive to buy these containers individually and to build up a set gradually.

£150–180

► By looking inside these two containers, you can find a useful clue to date them. The one on the left is self-coloured inside, which dates it from the early 1930s; it would have been bought plain and the lettering applied at home. The container on the right, with a white interior, was made between 1900 and the 1920s. Similar jars with raised white lettering and a pale blue interior were introduced in the 1930s; ones with flat lettering were available in the 1950s. Lids from both periods were self-coloured.

Left: £6–10 (£8–12 if plain) | **Right: £15–20**

HERBS & SPICES

Herbs are known to have been used since Roman times in the preparation of both food and medicines. By the Middle Ages, they were widely grown and used either to add flavour to unexciting food or to disguise tainted meat and game. Favourite ones included sage, parsley, fennel, mint and garlic. Typically, various types were put into a muslin bag, a *bouquet garni*, and added to stews and soups as they were cooked. Since herbs were so widely available and were simply used straight from the herb garden or dried in bunches and hung from the kitchen ceiling, storage jars were not needed.

By the 19th century, however, herbs had begun to disappear from general use in many northern European countries. The famous 20th-century British cook and writer, Elizabeth David, played an important role in bringing herbs back into fashion in Britain after World War II, with her hugely successful travel cookery books, such as *Mediterranean Food* and *French Country Cooking*, published in the 1950s. Her evocative descriptions of how herbs were used in Mediterranean cooking had an enormous impact on a country recovering from food rationing and were responsible for making herbs popular again.

▼ This blue and white mixed herbs jar is an example of Cornishware kitchen ware pottery, first produced in the 1930s by T.G. Green & Co., makers of household pottery since the mid-1860s.

£12–15

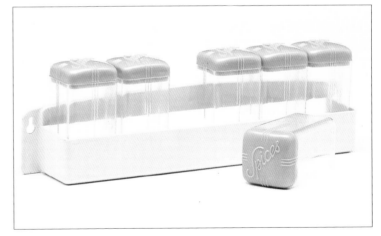

▲ These 1950s plastic spice containers have a useful hanging rack, although the jars themselves are not very practical, as they are very small and the plastic tends to be brittle and easily cracked. The spice jars were sold plain and the buyer could stick on specially produced name labels. The lids were made in various colours – look out for them in red, yellow and pale green.

£7–10

▼ Made c.1860, this pretty tin contains four black japanned tin spice containers and a nutmeg grater, neatly fitting into different compartments. Individual containers are often lost, so be sure to check they are original and that their lids fit snugly. They were also painted in other colours, such as red.

£100–120

▼ Originally, this set of four 1930s glass spice jars would have been kept in the inside rack of a kitchen cabinet door. The metal lids screw on to the jars and, if they have suffered any rust, this would lower the value. The jars should have a wax-covered card liner that fits under the lid for a closer seal. If the disc is missing, it is possible to use a double sheet of greaseproof paper cut to size instead.

£10–14 a set

◀ At one time, herbs and spices would have been stored separately; this Dutch hand-painted herb and spice storage rack produced from the late 1950s to the early 1960s illustrates how attitudes changed, as visual appeal became a priority. Mixed spice containers also became popular at this time. The choice of spices in this set is particularly curious. Why have only cloves and cinnamon?

£15–20

◀ Special spice containers were first made in the 17th century, often in the form of wooden cabinets with drawers or as small chests that stood on a table or hung on the wall. By the 1840s, these had developed into stacking spice columns – small round boxes that fitted on top of each other to form a 'tower'. This one has drawers for laurel and lemon, not commonly seen.

£120–140

▲ Possibly a souvenir from World War
II, when American soldiers were based
in Britain, this is a 1940s American
Army-supply cloves tin. Originally
containing whole cloves, it would have
been issued to the army's catering corps.
It is an unusual find, as it would never
have been available commercially.

£10–12

SALT JARS

Salt is one of the most important ingredients, used both for
preserving and for adding flavour to food when cooking. As
a precious commodity, great care was taken to store it
properly, where it would be kept dry as well as close at hand
when cooking or preparing food. Traditionally, salt jars were hung by
the hearth, where they were protected from damp, so they usually
have hanging hooks. Over the centuries salt jars have been made in a
variety of materials. Although earthenware versions were popular in
Europe in the 19th century, in America wood was preferred. Produced
in different types of wood, they were generally plain in design, apart
from those made by the Dutch settlers in Pennsylvania, which were
always elaborately carved and painted.

Britain made fewer wooden salt jars, and usually used only oak.
Rarely elaborate or carved, the earliest ones were made with leather
hinges – to prevent corrosion. By the 20th century, most salt boxes
were made from pottery, enamel or china. Ironically, they often had
metal hinges and so many have suffered much irreversible damage,
such as warping, while others have lost their original lids.

◄ Glass cannot be corroded
by salt and so makes an ideal
material for a salt storage
container. However, be
careful to check any glass
kitchenware carefully, as
items are greatly devalued if
cracked or chipped. Also,
check the wooden lid fits
snugly on salt jars such as
this one. This salt box was
made in France in the 1930s
for both the home and the
export markets, which is
why the manufacturers have
left a blank area on the front,
where a label could be
applied in any language.

£30–38

◄ It is rare to see this type of French painted tin salt box in such good condition. Remarkably, it still has its original wooden liner inside, which prevents the salt from corroding the tin and reducing the value. Note its hook: this 1920s box was made for hanging at the side of the range or stove.

£35–40

▲ The curved shape of this fruitwood salt barrel helps identify it as Scottish – English ones were usually square or rectangular. This one was made c.1870, but the design was produced until c.1910, using alternate light and dark woods to prevent shrinkage.

£130–150

► This reproduction glazed earthenware pig jar (also known as a salt jar or a salt kit) with white slip trailed decoration was made in the 1920s as a copy of those made in Sunderland in northern England in the early 19th century. Originally, these pig jars fitted into ledges in a fireplace to keep dry. They are possibly so-named because of their pig snout shape; the distinctive large opening makes it easy for cooks to reach in and take a handful of salt to add to the pot. Pig jars were not made outside England and so are rarely found in other countries today.

Early 20th-century reproductions can be easily distinguished, as they have 'SALT' spelled out, usually on the front of the jar – the word never appeared on earlier examples. Reproductions also do not have the typical crude finish of originals and the glaze is much more glossy. Do not be put off, however, as good-quality reproductions are still collectable.

£15–20

BREAD BINS

One of the earliest ways to store bread was to use large wooden frames, called bread flakes, suspended from the ceiling. Thought to have been introduced in the Middle Ages, hanging bread flakes kept bread above the floor and away from rats and mice.

By the mid-19th century, earthenware crocks were introduced, along with enamelled iron bread bins. By the late 19th century, stoneware bread crocks with tinplate lids were produced, and in the 20th century, as bread bins became popular, enamelled steel and painted tin bins were made in various colours and designs, similar to those available today.

No matter what material a bread storage container is made from, ventilation is always important, as air helps keep bread fresh for longer. Early earthenware bread crocks had efficient high domed earthenware covers with strap handles and ventilation holes beneath.

However, remarkably, from the 1950s onwards bread bins were often made without ventilation holes. As a result, bread could not be stored effectively, particularly commercially-made loaves. Wrapped in plastic bags, these loaves tend to 'sweat' if they are not ventilated and go mouldy in just a few days.

▲ As is often the case, this 'Improved Bread Pan' from 1880 has lost its perforated steel lid over the years. It is difficult to find a suitable replacement – bread boards fit, but do not allow ventilation. This one also has a severely chipped rim, which lowers value slightly, but it is more interesting than many, having been stamped with the name of the shop where it was bought: *FRAIN. CHINA MERCHANTS DUNDEE.*

£50–120

DOULTON & CO.
The firm were founded in 1835 in Lambeth, south London, and produced stoneglaze sewage pipes and sanitary and kitchen wares, such as the 'Improved Bread Pan' (above). In 1841 Henry Doulton, son of the founder, made a 300 gallon chemical jar, which was displayed at the entrance to the pottery with a notice claiming it was the largest stoneware vessel in the world.

The pottery gradually expanded to include terracotta sculpture and ornamental wares, especially vases and jugs, from the turn of the century. In 1902, the company were given permission to re-name themselves Royal Doulton.

▶ Made in the late 1920s, this white enamel bread bin with raised blue lettering is part of a series of storage containers. The matching blue handles are a nice touch and, although quite badly chipped on the lid, it is still an attractive item. It has no chips inside, so it could be used for storing bread.

£25–28

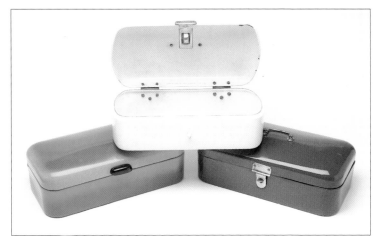

▲ These robust bread bins were used in both Holland and Germany from the 1890s to the 1940s (Holland still use them today). As well as these colours, they were produced in green and red. They should all have white interiors and most have a latch of nickel steel and ventilating holes at the back of the box allow the air to circulate.

By the 1950s, carrying handles were no longer added, as can be seen in the one on the left; other details remained the same. The one in the centre is an early example, dating from the 1900s. The deep blue colour of the 1930s box on the right is very unusual, making it particularly desirable.

£45–65 each

▶ This bread bin is green, a favourite colour in the 1930s. Although typical in shape and design of many bread bins produced from the 1930s to the 1950s, it has an unusual style of lettering.

£25–28

▲ 'Pride O-Home' was the slogan used by Homepride, a brand of the flour producers, Fosters. Established in the 1920s and originally known as Tommy Homepride Mills, Homepride factories were based in Cambridge, Coventry and Birkenhead.

Between 1922 and 1923 Homepride produced promotional kitchenware all marked with the 'Pride-O-Home' slogan, such as this highly collectable painted tin bread bin.

£25–30

▲ This type of painted aluminium cake tin was widely produced throughout the 1950s by firms such as Tala and Wessexware. Also available were biscuit tins and a combination stacking set for both cakes and biscuits, made in several colour combinations. A similar tin was produced in the 1930s. These earlier ones are easily distinguished, as they are of painted tin, heavier and have a hinged lid.

£10–15

▲ Although this biscuit tin is not marked with the name of any biscuit manufacturer, it is likely to have been sold as a gift item to be re-used afterwards for storage of other biscuits. Made in the 1950s, it is still in good condition, although the lid is not very airtight.

£6–8

CAKE & BISCUIT TINS

Afternoon tea had become an established institution among the British middle and upper classes by the mid-19th century. The ritual involved the preparation of numerous different types of cakes, biscuits and sandwiches by kitchen staff. As these tea parties were often attended as many as 30 people in the most wealthy households, food was always freshly prepared every day and there was generally no need for storage.

By the late 19th century, biscuits and cakes

▼ Part of a large series of hard-wearing enamel storage containers, this cake tin is rarer than the rest of the set (on p.19) and was made from the 1900s to the 1920s. The inside is white and the tin has raised white lettering. A similar, but darker blue, cake tin with flat lettering was made in the 1950s.

£25–35

were produced in increasing numbers by commercial bakeries. Popular luxuries, they were often sold in attractive tins, which were re-used afterwards for other storage.

By 1900, it was possible to buy tins specifically for storing cakes and biscuits, often in sets comprising different-sized containers for various kinds of homemade and bought cakes. Favourite cakes included Battenburg, ginger cake, fruit cake and the favourite 19th-century delicacy, the Victoria sponge cake.

Home baking continued to be popular throughout the 20th century, in spite of the success of leading brands, such as McVitie's (which became part of United Biscuits).

◄ Among the leading British biscuit makers of the late 19th/early 20th century were Meredith & Drew Ltd. Based in Scotland, they operated from the 1890s to the 1940s (when they joined United Biscuits). This glass jar from the 1920s would originally have been full of biscuits and kept on a shop counter to promote them.

£35–45

▼ The rubber ring on the flat wooden lid of this container would keep biscuits fresh for several weeks. Stamped 'Torquay-Devon Pottery Ltd.' on the base, it is a typical late 1950s/early 1960s design.

£10–15

▲ One of the most popular snacks ever produced, potato crisps evolved from a recipe brought over to Britain from France, by Carters, a wholesale grocery company in London. The idea appealed to the company's manager, Frank Smith, who developed the product for the firm with Mr. Carter, the proprietor. In 1920, Smith branched out on his own, setting up his own company, Smith's Potato Crisps Ltd., which became one of Britain's major crisps manufacturers. This Smith's crisps tin was made in the late 1920s and was an ideal way of selling larger amounts of crisps, for parties and picnics.

£20–30

WIREWORK
STORAGE
CONTAINERS

Wirework is thought to have been invented by Slovakian tinkers in the 18th century. Nomadic people, they travelled through the Austro-Hungarian Empire, selling everyday objects made from carefully twisted wire. Once the tinkers had settled in countries such as Germany, France and North America, they continued to develop the craft locally, producing a wide variety of useful household items, such as baskets, glass carriers and even dog muzzles.

Early wirework items, from the 1700s to the early 20th century, are beautifully made, with the wire twisted and turned into place. These pieces are highly desirable and can make a wonderful collection. It is wise to check carefully for any rust as this may make the wire brittle and prone to snapping easily when being cleaned. Examples,from the late 1930s onwards are far less valuable.

Later items can be easily distinguished, as the pieces of wire are heavier and usually welded or soldered together. Beware of wirework that has been artificially aged; the patina of the wire will not have the same depth of colour as earlier pieces.

▲ This Dutch galvanized steel and wire potato basket was used in the potato fields in the 1920s and 1930s. The basket would help riddle the dirt off the potatoes as it was carried along by two people. Similar ones were used in Britain.

£35–45

▼ This French wire glass carrier from the 1900s would have been found in cafés and bars. The waiter would use it to carry drinks outside and then to clear away the glasses afterwards.

£40–45

▼ A rare three-tiered vegetable stand from the 1900s, this piece has been designed to fit neatly against the wall. Made in England from galvanized steel wire and available in several sizes (and also in green), it is an ideal shape for storing vegetables, as the open shelves allow the air to circulate freely.

£40–50

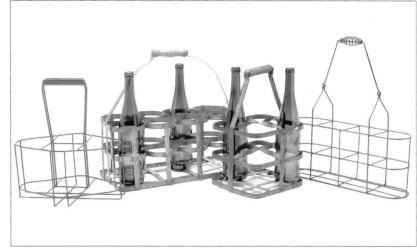

▲ Metal and wire wine-bottle carriers were popular in France from the late 19th century onwards and were made in various shapes. The one on the left, which dates from the late 1930s, is an unusual diamond shape. To its right is a later eight-hooped galvanized steel carrier from the 1930s to the 1940s, again an unusual shape and also larger than average. The four-bottle carrier next to it is a more common design. Made in the late 1920s, it has an attractive latticed bottom and is in good condition. The swing wire handle on the 1930s carrier on the right is unusual and its neat compact shape makes it very sought after, as it does not take up much space. Check condition: rusty metal reduces value greatly, although most collectors like pieces to have some wear and tear.

£25–50 each

► Made in France in the 1920s, this galvanized steel and wire basket would originally have been used by kitchen staff from cafés and hotels to carry fresh fish back from the market. Check the wire carefully, as the salty wet fish would often erode the metal until it snapped and many baskets have been crudely repaired.

Baskets of this type should always have a wooden handle; beware of a basket that does not, as it is likely the handle has been sawn off by an unscrupulous dealer to make it resemble a shopping basket.

£30–35

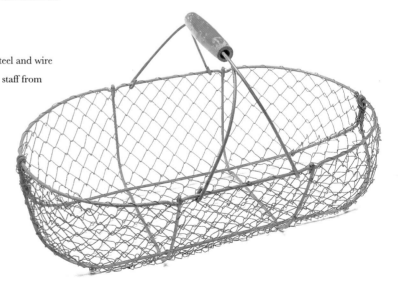

 This is a late Victorian meat safe, made of pine and with wire gauze panels on the front and side. Note how the safe is raised off the ground – rats and mice were still a problem for many households.

£100–125

MEAT SAFES & OTHER STORAGE

Before refrigerators were widely available, from the 1950s onwards, storing food was not easy in small houses that did not have room for large walk-in pantries. Food safes were the best method of storage, although they kept food fresh for only a few days.

In the early 19th century meat was generally stored in large wooden cupboards. These cupboards were mostly fairly plain in design, with simple holes cut out to keep the meat ventilated. Countries such as Hungary and Czechoslovakia in Eastern Europe made highly decorative versions, as did the Pennsylvania Dutch settlers in North America

REFRIGERATORS

The first domestic electric refrigerator, known in Britain as a fridge, is said to have been developed in a wash house in Indiana, USA, in the early 1900s. Following successful trials, over 50 fridges were built by 1919, when the inventors set up the Guardian Frigerator Company (later the Frigidaire Corporation). By 1923, the company had started manufacturing in Britain.

World War II halted the development of domestic refrigerators. Towards the end of the war, however, the British government undertook a massive building project to counter the problems of housing shortage as a result of German bombing. These temporary prefabricated houses (known as prefabs) were the first new houses to feature a built-in refrigerator in the kitchen. Until then, refrigerators had been considered a privilege of the rich.

The food freezer developed slightly later than the refrigerator, but was to become equally popular. One of the main protagonists was the American inventor and explorer, Clarence Birdseye, who, while on a hunting trip in Canada in 1923, noticed that fresh meat and fish exposed to arctic temperatures tasted fresh when thawed and cooked months later.

By the early 1960s, 22 per cent of British homes had a refrigerator and by 1969 this had risen to 56 per cent. As a result, meat and food safes were no longer used.

and the Welsh, who called them cheese cupboards.

Between the 1930s and the 1950s it became very popular in Britain to paint wooden furniture, particularly kitchen tables, cupboards and food safes. One reason was that good-quality wood was not available, because of shortages during World War II.

The only furniture manufactured at that time was 'utility' furniture, which, as the name suggests, was basic in style, design and material; pieces were often painted to make them seem more attractive.

In recent years, many painted wooden food safes have been stripped to suit the 'country cottage' look popular since the 1970s. Consequently, original painted pieces now command a premium, particularly with devotees of the 1930s and 1940s.

▲ Large painted pine cupboards, such as this, were used as general food safes for items such as cheese, butter and bacon. Made in the late 1930s to the early 1940s, this one would have been bought plain and painted by its owner. Pests such as rats were no longer so widespread, so the safe has no legs.

£65–75

► *Groenten* means vegetables in Dutch and this red enamel bucket would have been used to collect peelings and parings. It was made in the late 1920s (in black and green too) and it is unusual to see such buckets outside the Netherlands.

£25–30

◄ This glazed stoneware flagon can hold up to two gallons of any type of liquid, from vinegar to ginger beer. Made between the 1880s and the 1940s, they are easy to find, as many manufacturers produced them. This one is marked *Bunts L.-pool*.

£12–16

DAIRY

In the 19th century many families kept one or two cows for their own dairy produce and made their own butter and cheese in a dairy which was often adjacent to the house. Any excess would be taken to the local market.

When the butter had been churned, washed, worked and patted into shape by the dairy worker, it was marked with special motifs. To decorate the butter, either a carved butter print was used which was pressed down on the butter, or a roller was rolled over the butter to produce attractive designs on the surface.

Milk and cream were also delivered to nearby homes by a local farmer in a handcart. As cities and towns grew larger, a more sophisticated system for delivering milk was developed. By the late 19th century, large dairies, such as the Express Dairy in Britain, were established, which were able to deliver dairy produce every day.

Butter and cream tended to be made at home in Britain until the 1950s, but, along with cheese, could also be bought from local grocers and markets. Interestingly, in continental Europe there has never been any tradition of delivering dairy produce to the door.

▼ A wooden butter dish and knife from the 1890s.

BUTTER

Butter is made by agitating cream until it thickens. In the 19th century on farms where butter was made in large quantities and sold at market, various types of rocker-action churns were used in the dairy. The simplest was made of wood, shaped like a child's cradle and rested on carved rockers, while larger ones worked by means of a large wheel driven by a small dog or by water power from a nearby stream.

Once the butter was made, it was shaped using butter pats, usually made of wood. The pats were dipped in warm water and the lump of butter patted into a slab, usually 1lb (450g) in weight.

Curlers are used to shape butter into attractive individual curls; the end of the curler is dipped into hot water and drawn along the length of the slab. In the 19th century they were typically homemade out of horn or wood, but by the 20th century they were mass-produced and made of metal. Butter ballers work in the same way.

Domestic butter-making equipment was first used in the 1890s in North America and was available in Europe by the early 20th century. Home butter-making was popular until the 1950s.

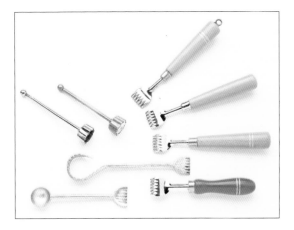

▲ This selection of butter curlers and small butter pat makers was produced between the late 1920s and the 1950s. This group includes four curlers with wooden handles (right) made by the British firm Nutbrown.

£5–10 each

▼ Dating from the 1920s, this French terracotta butter cooler comprises a base and a cover. The cover is hollow inside and has two holes at the top. Cold water is poured inside the cover and this keeps the butter cool underneath.

£25–30

▼ Traditionally, it was popular to decorate butter with attractive designs. Butter stamps were most commonly used and moulds such as these are more unusual. Surplus butter was sold by the farmer's wife at market and butter stamps acted as a trademark, distinguishing the butter from different farms. Stamps and moulds often depicted appropriate farm animals, crops and plants found on farms. Thus, a farm set in a valley might use a swan and bulrushes, while a farmer with a good herd might have a portrait of his prize cow.

£90–100

▲ This large butter dish would have been kept in the larder, rather than on a meal table, in a late Victorian household. The lid is hidden from view, resting on the bottom of the rim. Glazed white stoneware was very fashionable in the late 19th century and was used to make all types of useful storage containers.

£25–30

► By the 1930s, butter-making equipment had become quite advanced. Made between the 1930s and the 1940s, this butter churn features an unusual egg-shaped attachment on the lid, which allows air into the jar when the handle is turned.

£45–60

▼ This Pyrex butter dish has a white opalware base and clear cover with a crest motif. Made in the 1950s, it holds approximately ½lb (200g) of butter.

£5–10

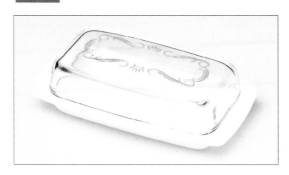

EGGS

Eggs were traditionally stored in open wire or willow baskets and hung from the ceiling of a larder, away from the rats and mice which would otherwise eat them. They were also kept on long wooden racks. From the mid-19th century onwards, egg racks became smaller (usually holding up to one dozen eggs) and new versions were made that could be stacked on top of each other.

Other types of egg storage included pottery hen nests. Introduced in the 1840s, they were produced in vast numbers by Staffordshire

▲ This rare English wirework egg basket was made in the 19th century and is of exceptional quality. The basket is strong and would hold several dozen eggs.

£70–100

▼ Egg separators are used to separate the yolk of the egg from the white. The separator on the left was made in the late 1940s and could also be used to lift boiled eggs from a pan.

£5–10 each

▲ Both decorative and practical, this early 19th-century egg stand is made from cast iron and wood. It would have been found in both town and country larders.

£200–250

potteries, originally filled with sweets as fairground prizes. Hen nests were also made in bone china or Parian ware (unglazed, fine-grained porcelain) and used to keep boiled eggs warm at the breakfast tables of middle- and upper-class Victorian homes.

As more people moved to cities and towns, it was necessary to find a way to transport eggs in large numbers without breaking them. One of the most original inventions was a special box with felt pockets inside to hold the eggs. These boxes ranged in size – the smallest could hold three dozen eggs, while the largest carried 35 dozen. Introduced in the 1890s, they were still used up to the 1930s.

▲ Hen nests were generally made from pottery, so this one, made in the 1930s, of amber glass, is particularly interesting. It has been cast from a mould and the details are clearly defined, particularly on the feathers.

£30–40

◄ As salads became increasingly popular in the 1930s, Tala launched the egg wedger, which, as the name suggest, cuts the egg into bite-size pieces. This version was made from the 1940s to the 1950s and still has its original box, adding to the value.

£8–12

► Painted tin egg stands were very popular between the 1930s and the 1950s. This one is by Worcesterware and was also made in red, white and green. Other makers included Tala and Wessexware. Stands by Wessexware have a wide handle, while, on Tala stands, the bottom tray can be taken out. Avoid those that have been repainted, as they are of little value.

£15–20

CREAM & MILK

In the 19th century most farms and large country houses had a dairy, and even small households in the country kept their own goat or cow – often known as 'house cows'. By the 1850s, dairies in Britain and North America started to deliver milk to homes in cities and towns. Initially, these dairies were built in cities, milking large herds of cows that were kept permanently indoors and fed on corn and hay brought in from the countryside.

The city dairy had disappeared by the 1920s and milk was sent to town by train in large churns. Farmers would take churns full of milk to the railway station every morning for the train to pick up, as well as delivering milk to local homes. Billycans (small churns) were left outside the house and the farmer would ladle the milk into it.

The use of milk bottles dates back to 1879, when the Echo Farms Dairy Company of New York, USA, first sold milk in glass bottles. In Britain, the Express Dairy, founded in 1874, carried out experiments in selling milk in wired-cap bottles, but abandoned the idea as it was too costly. By 1906, however, the use of glass bottles for milk had become widespread throughout Britain.

◄ Made in the 1940s, this is a jug and beater set. A versatile piece of equipment, it was claimed by its makers, Platers & Stampers, to 'beat eggs, cream and mix batter as never before, so efficiently and easy'. It is well-designed and all the different components fit together snugly to prevent splashing. This one has four beater blades, models were also made with eight. The set was produced, complete with a free recipe book, as part of the popular Skyline kitchen utensils series.

£20–25

▲ These two cream makers have similar names, but were made in the 1930s by different companies. The blue-specked octagonal 'Bel-Jubilee' cream maker (left) has a moulded translucent container and a 'Jacobean-style' glass receptacle (as described in the trade catalogue).

On the right is a 'Jubilee Empire' cream maker with a web glass container. These came in various colours – brown, green, dark red and bright red. Interestingly, in the 1930s the 'Bel' model was regarded as of superior quality and was more expensive, while, today, the 'Empire' is more sought after, because of its desirable mottled Bakelite top.

£12–15

▼ The equipment and utensils in this eclectic selection were all designed to prevent boiling milk from spilling out of a pan.

The milk saucepan on the left is a 'WHIS-I-MAGIC-MILK' pan made by the British manufacturers, Mirrorware, throughout the 1950s. It works by adding water to the funnel in the centre of the pan, and when the water boils inside a whistle blows to indicate that the milk has nearly reached boiling point and should be taken off the heat. Although ingenious, the pan is clumsy to use and difficult to clean.

A similar and equally imaginative design, the polished aluminium 'milk saver' in the centre was made in the 1950s. It is placed in the centre of a pan and the boiling milk sets the whistle off.

On the right is an enamel milk boiler made in France between the 1930s and 1940s. Its lid has holes in it and when the milk boils it bubbles through the holes to indicate it is ready! The boiler can also be used as a milk jug too.

Milk savers, such as the ones at the front, are added to a pan of milk and rattle when the milk is about to boil to attract the attention of the cook. The one on the left is French and was made in the late 1930s. They are still being produced today.

The small pottery milk saver on the right was made in England in the 1950s. The hanging ring allowed it to be hung by the kitchen stove between uses. This one was produced as a novelty item and it is more usual to find plain-coloured ones.

£5–15 each

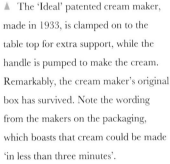

▲ The 'Ideal' patented cream maker, made in 1933, is clamped on to the table top for extra support, while the handle is pumped to make the cream. Remarkably, the cream maker's original box has survived. Note the wording from the makers on the packaging, which boasts that cream could be made 'in less than three minutes'.

£12–15 (with box)

ICE CREAM

Ice cream originated in the Far East, arriving in the West by the end of the 17th century. It was King Charles II who supposedly ate the first English ice cream in May 1671, following the fashion that had started on the Continent for *eaux glacés*, *eaux d'Italie* and *acque gelate*. It quickly became popular and at large feasts and banquets a refreshing sorbet would be served between each course, as a *digestif*.

The earliest ice cream was made from ice, milk and eggs in pewter pots with tight-fitting lids, and stored in special ice houses. By the early 19th century, there was a host of very elaborate pewter moulds from which to

WALL'S ICE CREAM

One of the most successful ice cream makers in Britain are Wall's, the first company to sell pre-wrapped ice creams from mobile ice cream tricycles. Introduced on 16 July 1922, Wall's ice cream quickly became popular, partly because of their imaginative marketing techniques. The slogan 'Stop Me and Buy One' soon became a familiar household phrase and Wall's also produced special cards marked with a 'W' which could be displayed in the front window of a house to notify the Wall's van that the family wanted to buy some ice cream.

In 1959, Wall's opened what was to become the world's largest ice cream factory, in Gloucester. Ice cream is still made there by Wall's, which are now a multinational firm. In 1981 they merged with Bird's Eye, becoming Bird's Eye Wall's.

► This conical ice cream server was made in America in the late 1870s. Inside the scoop are two blades and when the small screws at the top of the scoop are turned, the blades scoop out the ice cream cleanly.

£35–75

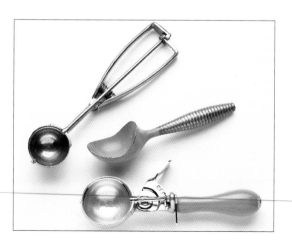

◄ These three ice cream servers show the variety of designs available in the mid-20th century and their different uses. The top one was made by Reliance in the mid-1930s, for commercial use. It has a spring-grip action and is still in production today.

The one in the centre was made in Italy in the 1930s and is also still produced today. Beware of new ones as they are of much poorer quality.

Tala made the spring-grip server (bottom) with the green wooden handle – it was also available in cream and yellow. This one was produced from the 1930s to the 1950s.

£5–20 each

choose, with intricate and varied designs, such as fruit, vegetables, birds and flowers.

The popular taste for ice cream owes its origin to the Italian immigrants who arrived in Britain in the second half of the 19th century. One of many famous ice cream makers of this period was Carlo Gatti, whose family firm made and sold Italian-style ice cream. Known as 'hokeypokey', it was offered in square slabs wrapped in white wax paper and eaten in glasses called penny licks. By the 1920s, the production of ice cream was a major industry, with many manufacturers. Ice cream also continued to be made at home throughout the 20th century and the utensils and equipment have not greatly changed over the past 100 years.

▲ The design of this American ice cream freezer made in 1900 was so successful that it has never been greatly changed. There are many brand names to look out for, such as Reliance's 'White Mountain Freezer' and Shepard's 'Lightning Ice Cream Machine', both made in North America – this one was produced by the Richmond Cedar Works, also an American company. The coopered bucket has a wooden cylinder in the middle, which is turned by a handle. The cavity between the wood and the cylinder is packed with ice and salt. The ice cream mixture is placed in the middle cylinder and rotated by turning a handle. Today, plastic components are available which fit the original design.

£70–100

▼ This beautiful pewter mould was made in 1868 and consists of three separate parts. The ice cream is packed into the centre and the lid and base are put on tightly. When the ice cream is ready to serve, the mould can be taken apart, leaving an attractively shaped dessert.

The registration mark is dated 11th July 1868, which indicates that the mould has been made from lead pewter, banned from the late 1860s onwards, because it was found to be poisonous – so never use this mould for making ice cream today.

Be prepared to pay handsomely for moulds like this too: they are very sought after.

£200–250

DRINKS

Since the 17th century, the taste for hot drinks such as tea and coffee has led to a wealth of specially produced equipment with which to prepare them. Coffee grinders have been made in numerous different shapes and sizes, from hand-turned grinders made from top-quality lignum vitae wood to simple metal versions.

Similarly, as other drinks, including chocolate, became popular, new utensils were produced, such as special mixers advertising the name of the drink manufacturer. Bournville were among the first British companies to produce cocoa powder, in 1908, which they claimed aided restful sleep. Other favourite hot drinks introduced in the 20th century include Horlicks, Ovaltine and Bovril, also hailed for their nutritional benefits.

Cool, refreshing drinks like lemonade and orangeade were also popular

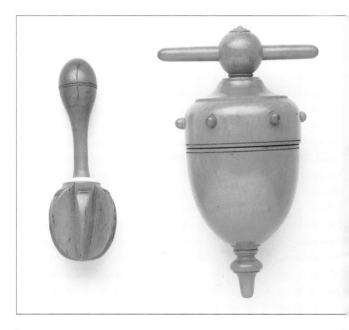

▲ Rare wooden juice squeezers made c.1830–1850.

homemade beverages. They required different utensils, including funnels and juicers, made from wood, metals, pottery, plastic and glass.

Other collectable drink gadgets include novelty items, for example cocktail mixers and ice crushers.

JUICERS & FUNNELS

Funnels were used for many kitchen activities, such as for funnelling lamp oil, jam, fruit fillings and drinks. Lamp and drink funnels tend to be among the earliest produced, dating from the early 19th century. By the late 19th century, however, funnels had a wider range of uses. In general, the size of the funnel is a good indication of its original use. Short wide funnels were suitable for jar-filling, while long thin funnels were best used for bottles with similar shaped necks.

Some funnels have a fine mesh disc at the top of the funnel tube, so it is likely that these funnels were used for filtering liquids.

Squeezers for oranges, limes and lemons were found in almost every kitchen from the late 19th century onwards as fruit juice was an important ingredient in cooking, as well as the base for homemade lemonade and orangeade. These squeezers were made of glass, and have remained unchanged.

Pottery squeezers, often in novelty shapes, were made in the 1920s and 1930s, while plastic ones mostly date from the late 1930s onwards. Look out for aluminium ones too – many were produced in North America.

▲ The mesh lemon squeezer on the left clips on to the top of a glass. It is a rare piece and has been intricately made. The larger aluminium lemon squeezer is British-made, by Solar in the 1920s. Squeezers with pip guards, such as this one, were more expensive than plain ones. Pip guards were useful labour-saving devices as they avoided the need to pour the juice through a strainer afterwards.

Left: £12–18   **Right: £10–14**

▲ This hardwood lemon and lime squeezer with pottery cups dates from c.1850 – note the hinges are made from brass so they would not corrode. Cups were also made from enamel or glass. This type of squeezer was also made in cast iron from the late 1870s to the 1920s; the cast iron was galvanized to stop corrosion.

£30–40

JUICER OR SQUEEZER?
In North America, any domed squeezer, where a lemon or orange is squeezed by hand over a dome, is known as a reamer. Those with hinged arms (usually of wood or cast iron with porcelain, enamel or glass inserts) are called squeezers. Mechanical devices, where the fruit juice is extracted by turning a handle, are known as juicers. In Britain it is simple, as they are all called squeezers.

▼ This rare large American squeezer was made in the 1940s and is marked 'Ade-O-Matic-Pat-Pending-Patent Applied-Genuine Corsta Porcelain'. It works on an armalian (spiral) mechanism and the top dome can be easily removed for cleaning.

£35–45

▲ Some juicers could be attached to a wall, such as this aluminium Speedo 'Super Juicer', made in America in the 1930s. Note that the bracket is missing, but a modern one can be used without depreciating the value.

£15–20

▼ These funnels were all made between the 1890s and the 1950s from a variety of materials. The oldest and rarest is the funnel on the far right, made in North America in the 1900s, specifically for stuffing a jam filling into Bismark cakes, a type of cake popular at this time and rarely made today. The most modern is the small white plastic salt funnel, offered as a promotional piece by the makers of Cerebos salt.

Under £5–16

▲ These two squeezers are made from urea formaldehyde, a type of plastic used to make a wide range of kitchenware. Urea formaldehyde is often mistaken for Bakelite, which is also mottled, but Bakelite was made only in dark colours, such as brown, red and green. In fact, Bakelite was seldom used for making kitchenware associated with preparing food, as it tended to give off an unpleasant smell and taint food.

£15–20

COFFEE GRINDERS

By the mid-18th century, coffee had became a favourite drink with the middle and upper classes (the only people who could afford to drink it).

Although coffee was ground by grocers in large cast-iron coffee mills, it also became fashionable to grind beans at home, using small wooden coffee grinders.

In 1815, the iron founder Archibald Kenrick patented a new box-type cast-iron coffee grinder. The coffee was put into the bowl at the top and when the handle was turned the blades ground the beans so they fell into the drawer at the base. Early grinders had brass or copper bowls. Always check the bowl is in good condition; it is the weakest part of the coffee grinder and prone to cracking or splitting.

The Kenrick coffee grinder design was copied by many other manufacturers and iron founders, such as Clark, Baldwin and Siddons until World War I and they are highly collectable today, particularly cast-iron wall-mounted grinders.

Coffee grinders did not change greatly in design during the 19th and 20th centuries and were produced by makers all across Europe and North America.

▲ 19th-century box-type coffee grinders produced by different companies were all fairly similar in design. The one on the left was made c.1860 by Baldwin, iron founders based in Southport in Lancashire, while the smaller one is by Kenrick. They produced grinders in various sizes, from the '000', the smallest (right), which can grind enough coffee for one cup, to the largest, 'No. 5', which can grind approximately three to four cups' worth. The size of the grinder is determined by the amount of coffee the drawer can hold. Kenrick coffee grinders always have the company's name on the front on a thin oval brass plate. Early ones are labelled Archibald Kenrick Iron Foundry, becoming Kenrick & Sons in the late 19th century.

£80–100 each

◀ It is rare to find a round grinder; most are square-shaped. This one was made by Siddons, a large iron foundry in West Bromwich in the heart of the Midlands in 1880. Siddons made far fewer coffee grinders than Kenrick, so they are particularly sought after today.

£150–170

► As coffee was still considered a major luxury in the 18th century, grinders were appropriately made of the finest materials and to the highest standard, using expensive woods such as mahogany. This mill is made from a rare darkly shaded wood known as lignum vitae and has been turned on a lathe into an elegant cylindrical shape.

£40–90

NORTH AMERICAN COFFEE GRINDERS

The major producers of coffee grinders from the 19th century onwards were the Enterprise Manufacturing Company of Philadelphia. Offered under the brand names American Coffee, Spice and Drug Mill, their grinders were originally intended for use by grocers and coffee dealers. Many were large in size and became a distinctive feature of many general stores.

▼ Coffee grinders did not change greatly during the 20th century. This one is French and was made from the 1920s to the 1930s. It has a wooden painted base, with a drawer into which the ground coffee beans fall, as in the 19th century

£25–30

▼ This coffee grinder is also French. Instead of wood, it is mostly made of painted tin, with a wooden surround and drawer. In spite of some paint chips, it is still in good condition and could be used today.

£25–30

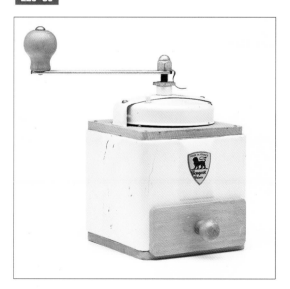

▼ Cocktails were very fashionable in the 1930s and a wealth of special utensils and implements were produced for making these drinks at home. This is an American aluminium 'Bar Boy' drinks measure, with a corkscrew and a bottle opener – the corkscrew fits neatly into the half-hollowed handle.

£12–15

OTHER DRINKS

All types of drinks were made at home, using a range of collectable utensils. Hot drinks were perennial favourites, with brands such as Ovaltine and Horlicks household names since the early 20th century. Both companies produced a range of equipment to use for making their drinks, which also became successful marketing tools, especially when they advertised the name of the manufacturer.

With the rise in popularity of cocktails, which had their heyday in the 1920s and 1930s, a range of equipment such as shakers, measures and mixers found its way into many homes in Europe and North America. These are very collectable today.

▼ Ovaltine can be prepared in specially produced glass mixers, such as this one from the 1930s. Ovaltine powder is put into the glass container with a little milk and mixed to a semi paste with the metal plunger – note the measures on the side. The paste is added to a pan of boiling milk, stirred and and the drink poured into a mug. Ovaltine produced this self-advertising mug in the 1950s, as a promotional gift.

£6–10 each

OVALTINE

Ovaltine is a Swiss product, originally created by a chemist, Dr. George Wander, from his early work in the 1860s. One of Ovaltine's most famous marketing techniques was the Ovaltiney Club launched in 1935. This was a special sponsored programme broadcast on Sunday evenings on Radio Luxembourg. The programme was suspended in 1939 when Radio Luxembourg closed for the duration of World War II and restarted in 1946, but broadcast for only a few more years. In 1975, the famous Ovaltiney song, 'We are the Ovaltinies' was given a new lease of life when it was used in a television commercial.

◀ Viandox is a French brand of meat extract, similar to the British brands Bovril and Oxo. This advertisement, which explains the nutritional benefits of the drink, would have been on display in a café or restaurant. The mug was made in the 1950s.

Advertisement: £7–10   **Mug: £8–12**

▲ To make hot chocolate frothy, an implement called a *molinillos* was traditionally used. They vary widely in design, from simple branches of bamboo to intricately carved versions from Mexico. This one is from Spain and was made in the 1950s. The *molinillos* was placed in a pan of melted chocolate and milk and its stem rubbed between the palms of the hands. The chocolate and milk quickly blend into a frothy cream, similar to a milkshake.

£7–10

▶ This Oxo mug was made specifically for the French market in the 1950s as a promotional item, although similar mugs were produced in other countries. The Oxo cube was first made in 1910, developed from a concentrated meat extract invented by a German chemist. They were not aluminium foil-wrapped until the mid-1950s.

£6–9

▲ Horlicks produced different-sized drink mixers. The one on the right dates from the 1930s, the other two were made from the 1940s to 1950s. The promotional mug is from the 1960s.

£6–14 each

HORLICKS

Horlicks was named after its inventor, James Horlicks, a pharmacist. Originally Scottish, he moved to the USA to join his brother in 1873. Together, they opened a firm in Chicago, specializing in making artificial infant food. In 1883, they registered a patent for 'malted milk'.

James Horlick returned to Britain in the early 1890s and opened a Horlicks factory in Slough, concentrating production solely on the malted milk drink. As with Ovaltine, it was marketed as a pre-bedtime drink and the company boasted that it prevented 'night starvation' and ensured a good restful sleep.

BAKING

Unlike modern kitchens, the main kitchen area in Victorian households had no built-in work counters. Instead, baking and other food preparation took place on a large, centrally positioned wooden table, usually made of deal or pine, which was scrubbed clean every day. Shallow drawers for baking utensils were incorporated in the table and as it was lower than a modern work surface, it was better suited to strenuous activities such as kneading dough.

By the mid-19th century, when cast-iron coal- or wood-burning ranges were introduced (see also p.78), there was a growth of equipment for baking as the ranges enabled more sophisticated cooking and baking techniques.

A wide range of utensils were used for baking from the 19th century onwards, such as earthenware mixing bowls, flour dredgers and rolling pins. Elaborate pies, jellies and other desserts were created from exotic moulds, while simpler baking tins and patty pans were used to produce a wealth of bread, cakes and biscuits.

In the first half of the 20th century there was a craze for tea parties where dainty sandwiches, cakes and pastries were served. A host of implements and baking tins were developed for making these treats.

▼ Two kugelhopf cake moulds.

MIXING BOWLS

Pottery was not widely produced in Britain from the end of the Roman occupation in AD 476 to the 16th century. Instead, most household utensils were made of wood, such as elm or sycamore.

By the mid-17th century, the most important British potters were based in Staffordshire. Different types of pottery were produced, particularly earthenware, which is very durable. The range of items was vast and included mixing bowls in varying sizes, as well as jars, plates and jugs.

Mixing bowls were also made for the rest of the British Isles, and pieces were exported to New England and Maryland in North America as early as 1653. Ceramics were not produced much in North America until the early 19th century, when the industry developed, mainly on the East Coast, in Philadelphia and New Jersey.

Mixing bowls on both sides of the Atlantic were generally plain in design. North American bowls of the early 19th century were were often plain red, white or yellow, with simple glazes. By the mid-19th century stripes of colour were added in both Britain and North America as well as elements of decoration. Late 19th-century bowls often had lips added too for pouring and were often made of cream earthenware or stoneware.

▼ This 19th-century mixing bowl should not be confused with a pancheon, a deeper bowl which is used for the mixing and rising of yeast dough. This style was unchanged for over two centuries, so dating is difficult. A shallow version of this bowl, with widely flaring sides was used for setting cream.

£45–65

▼ Many Victorian bowls, including this one, were not marked with the makers' name. The lip on this bowl would have been used to pour out batter mixture for recipes such as Yorkshire pudding. Always test a mixing bowl for cracks before buying – the bowl should give a good clear 'ping' when tapped with a pencil. Earthenware bowls were not fired at as high a temperature as china bowls and are not so strong.

£25–35

▼ Enamel mixing bowls were made in various sizes, from 5½ to13inches (14 to 33cm). This one is the largest size and can hold up to 2lb (900g) of flour and ingredients and is known as a chef's bowl. Dating from the early 1900s, it is rare to find one in such good condition. They were prone to being scratched inside by forks or whisks.

£18–24

▲ These mixing bowls all are all slightly different, which help to identify and date them. The buff colour of mixing bowls dates back to the 19th century, but over the years there were slight variations in tone, changing from a pearly white to a more creamy colour inside, while the outside colour became a deeper buff colour. Another 20th-century feature was the gripstand, which makes it easier for a cook to hold a bowl steady while mixing. The bowls at the back of the group all have gripstands and date from the 1930s to the 1950s. Main manufacturers of this type of mixing bowl include Mason & Cash and T.G. Green & Co. (also makers of Cornishware kitchenware).

£10–20 each

PATENTS

Patents provide useful clues for dating items. Since the late 16th century, the British Crown has granted letters patent to inventors protecting for a limited period their exclusive right to manufacture their inventions and to prevent other makers from copying the idea without redress.

It is possible to check a patent number of a product at the Patent Library in London, which keeps records of all the patents issued over the past 150 years. Their records will also state to whom the original patent was issued and on what date. However, remember that the date a patent was originally issued is not always the same as the age of the piece, as kitchenware products were often produced over long periods.

▲ Both these mixing bowls are made from earthenware. The one the left was produced by Lovatt's Potteries (established 1895) in the 1930s. It has been stamped in black 'Lovatt's England' on the base, indicating it was made after 1900; in the 19th century it would have been impressed into the bowl.

Although similar to T.G. Green's Cornishware pottery, the blue and white bowl was sold by Chefware as a less expensive alternative to Cornishware throughout the 1950s.

Left: £8–13 **Right: £5–8**

PUDDING BASINS & OTHER BOWLS

The simple wooden receptacles used in the Middle Ages had developed by the 19th century into tin, earthenware and metal bowls adapted to a wide range of uses, including warming, cooling, salting and storing food.

The British are traditionally known for their enjoyment of sweet and savoury steamed and boiled puddings, such as steak and kidney pudding, treacle pudding and spotted dick. These puddings, which have been on the menu in many homes since the mid-19th century, are made in special china bowls, to withstand the heat of steaming. To use a pudding basin for cooking, the bowl is first lined with suet pastry and filled with steak and kidney or shin beef. Basins can also be filled with syrup or stewed fruit at the base. After adding the filling, the pudding is sealed with a lid of suet dough or sponge mixture and covered with a lining of greaseproof paper.

The top of the basin is then covered with a cloth, which is tied under the rim of the basin with string. The opposite ends of the cloth are knotted to make a lifting handle suitable for taking the pudding in and out of boiling water. From the 1900s to the 1950s it was possible to buy special pudding cloths, made of cotton or linen, which are collectable providing they are not stained.

▼ Made in the 1930s by Joblings, these Pyrex dishes were produced in various sizes from 1 pint (0.6 litre) to 2½ pints (1.5 litres). The two flat-sided glass dishes are used for making soufflés or mousse. The other bowl is a pudding basin.

Under £5 each

▲ Sutox was a type of suet used as one of the main ingredients in steam puddings and this Sutox basin would have been offered as a promotional item in the 1930s. Made of aluminium, its main feature is a clip-on lid, which avoids the need to use greaseproof paper and cloths.

£8–10

◀ In the 1900s, butchers would sell potted meat in enamel advertising dishes such as this, as a way of promoting their name. Dishes were also made in white earthenware and would be kept by cooks after the meat had been eaten, as they could be re-used to make individual pies.

£35–45

▼ This highly sought after ironstone china 'Quick Cooker' by Grimwade's was made in 1911, although the design was first patented and introduced in 1909. It is an impressive advertising piece, promoting a whole host of products by Grimwade's, such as pie dishes, 'Safety Milk Bowls' and 'hygienic household jars'.

Directions on how to use the 'Quick Cooker' are printed on the top of the lid, where it also claims to cook the contents quickly from the centre to the circumference, with no pudding cloth required. The notches on the four points of the lid correspond to the four notches on the underside base. This is where string is tied.

£75–85

▲ Early Pyrex glass is generally cloudy in appearance as can be seen in the 4oz (100g) bowl on the left. Made in the 1930s, it was part of the 'Pyrex Oven Table Glassware Series'. The pudding basin is also made by Pyrex. Available in the 1930s, this one holds up to 1 pint (0.6 litre).

Under £5 each

▶ All these white earthenware pudding basins were made between 1910 and the 1950s. Note the way the colours vary in tone – by the 1950s they had changed from pure white to a more creamy colour. A clue for dating basins is that earlier ones are narrower and often have a curled edge, to allow string to be tied securely under the pudding cloth. Bowls with a deeper turned edge are usually earlier too.

£5–8 each

MEASURING JUGS

Among the earliest known household measures were wooden mugs. Commonly found in the 18th century, they were used to measure all types of foodstuffs, from liquids to potatoes, butter or nuts, and were made in varying sizes.

By the late 18th century, measures for specific items were available. Pewter measures were most commonly used for ale and vinegar, while earthenware ones were suited for milk and cream. Tin measures weighed shellfish, while corn was measured in deep round wooden containers.

With the advent of domestic household scales in the mid-19th century (see p.58), measures were used less, apart from wooden corn measures and measures for ale, milk and other liquids.

WEIGHING UP

Since the Middle Ages, the English system of weights and measures has been based on a single grain of wheat and, from the 16th to the 19th century, the standard pound was equivalent to 7,000 grains of wheat – known as the avoirdupois pound. In 1824, the official standard was changed to the Troy pound, weighing 5,760 grains. This new measure was not popular and was replaced in 1878 by the Imperial Standard Pound, which once again was 7,000 grains.

In continental Europe, the metric system of measuring has been in operation since the 19th century and the kilogram has traditionally been defined in terms of a prototype kept at the International Bureau of Weight and Measures (established in 1875) at Sèvres in France.

In North America, special-sized cups are used for cooking, evolved from using household cups and goblets. By the late 19th century, the size of a cup had been standardized to equal 8oz (225g).

▼ Made in the 1950s, the Cook's Measure (left) 'weighs and measures at a glance', according to the makers, Tala. Each row of measurements lists the range of items that can measured or weighed. Take care when cleaning this type of measure, as the paint comes off if a scourer or abrasive cleaner is used. The measure on the right, called the Cook's Treasure Measure, is an earlier version, from the late 1930s. Unpainted inside, it is slightly less easy to read, but contains just as much measuring information. Similar measures are produced today, but only in plastic.

£8–10 each

▶ Hardwearing but lightweight, aluminium is an ideal material for measuring jugs. One of the leading 20th-century makers were Swan Brand, which made the two jugs on the left. Bakelite collectors would be attracted to the jug , with a Bakelite handle (top right).

Far less desirable is the small jug in front. Made by Diamond Brand in the 1920s, it has a clumsy handle.

£5–10 each

▼ Glass was widely used for measuring jugs. The 2 pint (1.2 litre) jug on the left was made in the 1950s and is unusually large; ½–1 pint (0.3–0.6 litre) jugs are more common. Made from Pyrex, it is a strong household jug and can easily withstand hot liquids. Pyrex jugs are easy to distinguish, as the name is always impressed on the base.

The measurements on the jug in the centre include imperial, metric and American cups. Measurements on jugs have been both metric and imperial since c.1900, but few included American cups until the 1930s.

Oddly, the jug on the right does not have a handle, just a finger grip, and can measure up to 10oz (283g).

£8–12

▲ These three late 19th-century tin measures would have been used by shop keepers or merchants to measure out liquids or food for customers. To prevent any chance of under-measuring, each one has been officially stamped with its size by the British Customs & Excise department.

Large: £18–25 **Small: £18–20**

▲ When buying a measuring jug, make sure the measurements are clearly marked. Enamelled jugs, such as this from 1910 are becoming more difficult to find, especially in good condition.

£8–13

57

KITCHEN SCALES

Leonardo da Vinci (1454–1519), designed the first self-indicating scale. As with many of Leonardo's ideas, no practical application of the design was ever developed and it was not until the 19th century that self-indicating scales were made.

Before buying a set of kitchen scales, always test its accuracy. To do this with counter balance scales, put equal sets of weights on the scale – one on the weights side and one in the pan to check that they balance. If they are spring-type scales, simply put a weight in the pan.

▲ Although the manufacturers of these late 19th-century counter-balance scales with tin pans are unknown, the principle of their design is renowned. These types of scales were discovered by Professor Gilles Personne de Roberval in 1669 in France and are known as 'Static Enigma'. This means the machine oscillates above and below its normal level before coming to rest when it is balanced. This principle was widely adopted by scale makers and is still used today.

£30–35

▼ Salters have been among the leading international designers and manufacturers of scales since 1760. Based in West Bromwich, in the West Midlands, they introduced spring balance scales, which avoided the need for weights in 1770. One of Salters' most interesting inventions was the quadrant balance, such as this one, so called because of its shape. These scales were described in the Salters' catalogue of 1876 and it seems probable that they were produced in smaller numbers than the more usual circular, oblong or pedestal types, as they are very rare today.

▲ Always make sure that the scales still have a complete set of weights, heavier weights are the easiest to find individually. Most weights are made of cast iron, although some firms made the smallest ones, $\frac{1}{4}$oz (7g) and $\frac{1}{2}$oz (14g), in brass. These late Victorian scales are missing the two smallest weights. Typically, scales such as these would be able to weigh from $\frac{1}{4}$oz to 2lb (7 to 900g). Note the original paint is still on some of the weights.

£25–28

£40–60

WEIGHTS

Most Victorian weights were made of cast iron and brass, widely available, durable and inexpensive to produce. Other materials, such as stone, were occasionally used, particularly in the heavier ranges. Pottery weights were also made and are highly sought after today as they are much rarer. They were declared illegal in 1907 because of their tendency to chip and become lighter than their stated weight.

▲ Most 19th- and early 20th-century household scales were painted in drab colours, so these blue ones are particularly desirable, especially with their attractive Art Nouveau design. Made by a Germany company, Krups, well-known makers of kitchen spring balances in the early 20th century, they were produced specifically for export. The dial of these scales is made of vitreous enamel, as is the pan.

£35–40

► This version of Salter's spring balance household scales, made from the 1920s to the 1930s, has a small screw which can be adjusted to ensure complete accuracy of the needle. When a load is added the pressure pushes the springs down and the needle marks the weight on the dial. These can weigh up to 28lb (12.6kg).

£28–35

◄ These beam-balance kitchen scales with a chrome pan were made by Tower in the early 1960s, and offer a high degree of precision. They work by sliding two weights along a calibrated double beam until the beam is level.

£20–25

WEIGHING UP
BEAM SCALES   Pans are hung from the ends of a beam supported at the centre.
SELF-INDICATING SCALES   Scales on which the weight is displayed on a chart.
SPRING BALANCES   Scales which depend on springs as the resistant: often the weight is displayed on a dial.
COUNTER-BALANCE SCALES   Scales which use different–sized weights to counter- balance the weight of an object.

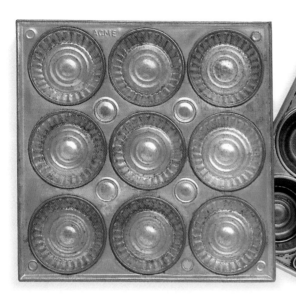

◀ One of the most appealing characteristics of tinware is the attractive patina that it acquires as it ages.

Remarkably, both these baking tins date from the 1930s; the one on the left looks brand new as it has been stored in a cupboard unused. Note the makers' name, Acme. They were major British manufacturers of all types of useful household utensils, from the 1920s to the 1950s.

£5 or under each

BAKING TINS

Tin has been available in Europe and North America since the mid-19th century. In North America it was initially fairly expensive and was highly treasured.

Local tinsmiths were known as white smiths to distinguish them from iron-workers. Some tinsmiths decorated the bases of tin items, including baking tins, on request; these are highly sought after today.

If you intend to use any early steel, tin or cast-iron baking ware, it is important to remember that care is needed to look after them. After use, baking tins should not be left to soak in washing-up water as they will rust, they should be washed carefully and dried immediately with a clean tea towel and stored in a dry place.

▼ Established in c.1910, H.J. Green & Co. Ltd. were a company of grocers suppliers, based in Brighton, Sussex. In the late 1920s they offered a range of promotional kitchenware, embossed with their company name and the name of one of their products. Today, they are still fairly easy to find and can be built up to make complete sets.

Flan tins: £4–6 each
Tartlet tins: £12–15 with box & booklet
Sandwich tin: £7–10   **Sponge finger tin: £10–15**

60

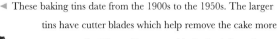

These baking tins date from the 1900s to the 1950s. The larger tins have cutter blades which help remove the cake more easily. The earliest cutter blades (top) from the 1930s are quite crudely made – flimsy and thin, with the blade sticking out from the edge of the tin in an unattractive way. By the late 1930s, the design had been refined and improved; the cutter blade on the bottom left tin is wide and folds neatly over the outline of the rim. The other sandwich tin is also from the 1930s and has a fluted rim.

Two types of tartlet tins are shown. The three darker ones (top) were made in the early 1900s. Of excellent quality and hard-wearing, they are far more desirable than the two lightweight 1950s ones below.

£5 or under each

▶ Although tins were often made for one specific purpose, they could also be used for other tasks. These two tins were made for Yorkshire puddings, but could also be used for making individual sweet or savoury pies. Again, the decline in quality over the years is evident. The tray on the left was made in the 1920s and has seamless cups, while the other, a 1950s tray, has been stamped from a single piece of metal. These tins are not marked, but brands include Peter Pan, Tala, Ovenex, Evaware and Bakejoy.

£5 or under each

◀ Made in the 1920s, the nine-cup embossed tin (right) was produced with considerable craftsmanship. Distinctive features of these tins include raised embossed seamless cups. The frame was made separately with holes for the cups. Individual moulded cups were pressed into the frame and double-seamed in. By contrast, the 12-cup tin from the 1950s has simply been stamped out of one sheet of tin. The detail in the embossing is not so detailed nor of high quality. Similar tins are produced today.

£5 or under each

The term 'patty pan' is derived from the French word, *pâte* meaning paste, although they were used to make English tartlets. From the late 19th century onwards, patty pans would be placed on baking sheets made from iron or heavy steel to bake in the oven. Early baking sheets are very hard to find today and are highly sought after. Patty pans are more widely available; early ones (from the 1890s–1940s) are usually made from heavy tinned steel, while later ones are much lighter. The small oval brass plate is a guide to using a 'regulo' thermostatic control, perfected by Radiation Ltd. in 1923. Today, the temperature control on gas cookers is still called the regulo.

Patty pans: £5–8 set of six | **Baking sheet: £5 or under**

Small cakes and tarts could be made in a range of pretty tins. Originally known as cornet moulds and later as cream horns, these jam and cream-filled pastries were perennial favourites. The boxed set of six cream horns was made by Tala (centre) in the late 1940s to the early 1950s, and to its right is a set of cornet moulds from the 1920s.

Popover pans (right of cornet mould), for small batter puddings, must not be confused with dariole pans (left of Tala box). The name 'dariole' refers to a traditional English cake of this shape, which was made from puff pastry and filled with custard. Both pans are collectable, especially in sets of six.

The set of brioche tins on the far right was made in the early 1900s and they are more desirable than the later tinned steel versions from the 1950s (far left).

The aluminium eclair moulds (front right) look brand new, but were made by Nutbrown in the late 1930s. These tins can also be used for baking *langues de chats* (cats' tongues), a type of flat oval biscuit.

Early boat moulds (front left), also known as *bâteau* or *barquette* moulds, are highly collectable today, especially when made of heavy tinned steel, such as these from the 1920s.

£6–14 a set

► From the latter part of the 19th century to the 1950s, baking tins were produced in a variety of shapes for different types of baking and cooking. The large, heavy oval tin, measuring 11 x 8in (28 x 20cm) could be used to make a large pie or to roast a piece of meat. It was also available in other sizes; 12 x 9in (30 x 22cm) or 13 x 10in (33 x 25cm).

To its right is a Russian cake tin by Tala. This tin has an additional piece that slots in the centre enabling different coloured sponge cakes to be made – the basis of a Russian cake or Battenberg as it is also known.

The small oval tin is a Charlotte mould. Used to make a French Fruit or Charlotte pudding (stewed fruit covered with layers of bread and butter), it was also available in a round shape and in various sizes – this one would make enough for two people.

Although the large square tin was primarily for making Yorkshire pudding, it could also be used to make parkin (a type of sticky cake made from oatmeal, treacle and ginger). As with much kitchenware, baking tins are versatile pieces of equipment.

£5–15 each

▼ Loaf tins were first made from the early 19th century, but afforded only by large, wealthy households. In most homes bread would be moulded by hand and baked in the oven on an iron sheet or earthenware dish.

By the turn of the century, tins were more widely available and were used for cakes, such as fruit loaf, too. Early 20th-century loaf tins, from the 1900s to the 1920s, tend to be of better quality than later ones and are more desirable. The two tins (centre and bottom left) were made from the 1930s to the 1950s.

The larger 2lb (900g) tin has a small hoop to hold when taking it out of the oven. The smaller one is marked Ovenex, a trademark of Platers & Stampers.

The two other tins date from the 1900s to the 1920s, are of better quality and have been wired around the rims to give them strength.

£5–8 each

◀ Sadly, the four 'heartlets' needed to complete this baking set by Tala have been lost over the years. The large heart is still in good condition, however, and the colourful original packaging adds greatly to its appeal. Although this one was made from the late 1950s to the early 1960s, they were first produced 20 years earlier and are still made today. When collecting boxed sets, always remember to check carefully that all the pieces are still intact.

£10–15 a set

▶ The style of graphics on this packaging, together with the wording, 'For Novel Moulded Dainties', gives a good indication that these flan tins were made in the 1930s (although they are still made today). The word 'dainties' was widely used in Britain to describe small fancy cakes and it was common for people to go to a tea-shop and ask for 'a pot of tea and a plate of fancies'!

£10–14

▼ The Swiss Roll tin on the left from the 1930s promotes Bird's 'Spongie Mix', first introduced in the 1920s. Kitchenware that advertises products made by Bird's is particularly sought after in North America. On the right is a French madeleine tray from the 1890s.

Left: £14–16   **Right: £15–18**

BIRD'S

Alfred Bird began his career as an 'experimental chemist', as he called himself, in Birmingham in 1837, at the age of 24. However, it was for convenience foods that Bird was to become most famous, in particular an eggless cornflour-based custard. Bird had originally made the custard for his wife, Elizabeth, who suffered from digestive problems and could not tolerate eggs.

RAISED PIE MOULDS

Raised pie moulds produce attractively decorated pie crusts and were traditionally used for poultry and game pies. From the late 18th century onwards game pies were made in earthenware moulds or tureens. Some were embossed with hunting emblems, and handles were sometimes moulded to represent a hare. Metal moulds originated in the 1850s to the 1860s and early ones often had elaborate decoration.

The raised game pie mould on the left was made in France from the 1870s to the 1900s and is oval in shape. The other is round and was made in Britain from the 1890s to 1900s.

Left: £30–40 **Right: £30–35**

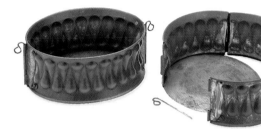

Cooling racks, or pastry trays as they are sometimes known, developed from the 1900s onwards. Note the decorative wirework gallery side on the large tray (front left) – to prevent cakes from falling off! By the 1920s, similar ones were available in France, with a mesh base, and, in the 1930s, they were also made by Tala. The chequered wire rack (top right) from the 1930s also has gallery sides, but they are much plainer in design and less attractive. Most pastry trays were made of lightweight re-tinned wire. However, the one on the top left from the 1930s to 1940s is made from a heavy galvanized steel. By the 1950s racks had become simple, strong and functional; the example on the bottom right typifies these characteristics.

£5–25 each

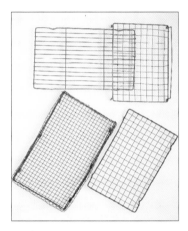

Cooling racks could be pretty as well as practical. The small daisy-shaped looped tinned-wire cake stand was made in France in the 1930s. The wire has been carefully curled and turned around a cross-shaped frame to produce a high-quality piece of wirework. It is so well made that it is possible that the cake would have been presented on it at the tea table.

The two larger racks were also made in France; the one on the right is the oldest. It was made in the 1930s and is more valuable as the wire has been weaved over the frame. The other rack was made in the 1950s and is identical to those produced today.

£5–15 each

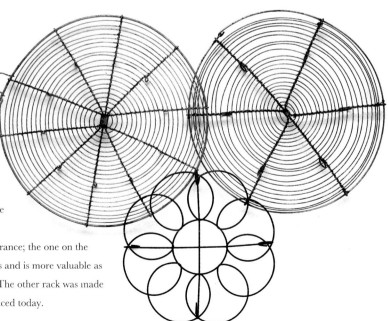

BAKING UTENSILS

A whole host of different utensils are used for baking. Many date back centuries and have been modified and improved over the past 100 years by commercial manufacturers. Biscuit cutters and pastry brushes are unchanged since 1800, conversely, icing kits are a 20th-century phenomenon.

◄ Remarkably, this packet of rice paper has survived intact from the early 1950s. Made of edible rice starch, rice paper is used when making meringues or macaroons. Before it was introduced in the 1920s, strong white paper was used, which had to be peeled off after cooking.

Under £5

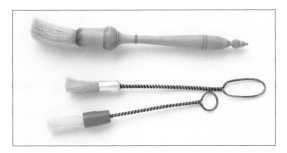

▲ Pastry brushes or glazing brushes date from the 19th century and are used for glazing pastry on pies with beaten egg yolk half a minute before the pie had finished cooking. If a lighter glaze is required, the whole egg with a little milk is used. Often, two brushes are needed, one for glazing and the other to grease plates and dishes before baking. The wooden-handled brush (top), from the late 19th century, is particularly well made; the handle has been turned on a lathe and the bristles are natural hog's hair.

Once brushes were commercially produced, less expensive versions were available. Made in the 1930s, the brush in the centre of the picture has a simple wire handle and an aluminium sliding finial that allows the bristles to be washed after use.

The one below is a 1940s version; the finial is made of plastic and it has a nylon brush head. Both were made by Betterwear (1929–present), major producers of all types of household items and pioneers of door-to-door selling.

£5–14 each

▼ These batter whips from the 1930s to 1950s are just a small selection from the wide range available during this period. The wooden-handled whips all carry the brand name Skyline, a trade name of the British manufacturers Platers & Stampers. The earliest dates from the 1930s and has a green and yellow handle and a distinctive 'new style' blade. Below is an oval whip with diamond-shaped perforations, made in 1938. Larger blades were popular by the 1950s and the blade on the chrome-plated whip (bottom) has been etched 'curved to fit the bowl'. The tinned steel 'Kitchamajig' whip (top) was made in the 1940s.

£6–9 each

▲ Locally made in Germany in the mid-19th century, this rare hand-carved wooden board is known as a bread slip. It was traditionally used by bakers for raising bread dough and for sliding loaves into the oven. Note the dark stains – from moist dough. The edges of the board are singed from where they have caught the heat of the oven. These imperfections add to its appeal.

£30–40

▼ In France long baskets are used to raise and prove the bread dough before baking. This 1930s wicker basket is lined to prevent the dough from sticking.

£18–24

◄ Hard woods are ideal for pastry boards as they are less likely to split or splinter than soft woods, although marble, aluminium, enamel and even glass have also been used.

The first pastry boards were used in the kitchens of large houses in the 17th century. These were long wooden boards that would have been put on top of a table. Smaller pastry boards were introduced in the 20th century as kitchens became smaller.

Although wood is difficult to date precisely, pastry boards tend to show signs of years of usage, such as knife marks and a greasy feel from where fat has soaked into the wood. These boards were made in the late 1920s to 1930s.

Small: £4–6   **Large: £7–10**

► Pastry crimpers, wheels, trimmers and jiggers are all names for types of tools that can make attractive decorated twisted edges for the pastry of pies and tarts. The wooden one (top) dates from the turn of the century and is made from hand-carved boxwood.

The other three are Nutbrown products. Still in its original box, the pie crimper second from the top was made in 1927, according to its patent number and the style of packaging. The other two are the same patented model; the green-handled one is from the 1930s, while the red-handled one is from the 1950s.

Top crimper: £8–12   **Boxed crimper: £5–8**
Loose crimpers: £5 or under

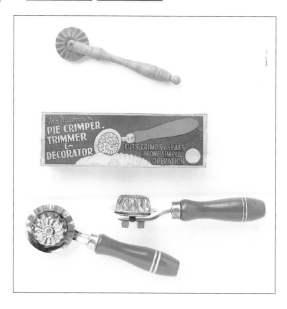

Sets of pastry cutters in green-painted hinged-lidded tins were produced by Tala in the early 1930s. Later in the 1930s pastel colours became available with a glossier finish. By the 1950s, the tins were made of light aluminium, in garish colours. The cutters were available either crinkly-edged or plain for the same price, and each tin contained four different-sized cutters, fitting neatly into each other.

Tin with set of cutters £10–14

▲ Made by Tala, in the late 1940s to early 1950s, the animal shapes in this set of six biscuit cutters, each featuring the Tala mark, include a pelican, seal, penguin, elephant, horse and hippo. It is rare to find a complete set with its original box. The base of the box has recipe instructions for biscuits.

£12–16 with box

◀ Although less durable and more brittle than metal, plastic was regularly used to make pastry cutters by the 1950s. Commonly sold through Betterwear salesmen, the cutters were available in a variety of pastel shades, including pink, blue, yellow and green.

£5 or under

▶ This set of novelty biscuit cutters by Nutbrown from the 1950s, complete with original box, includes a man in the moon, a star and a flower. These deep cutters could also be used to make fancy sandwiches.

Fierce competitors, Tala and Nutbrown would produce identical products and often the only way to tell the difference is to check for a makers' mark; both companies marked every item with their name. Nutbrown began as Thomas M. Nutbrown in 1927, registering himself as Thos. M. Nutbrown in 1932. The company closed in 1988, but Nutbrown products are now made by Fiskars UK Ltd.

£10–14 with box

▲ This gingerbread man cookie cutter was made in the 1950s by the American Aluminium Goods Manufacturing Co., specialists in novelty items.

£5 or under

PASTRY CUTTERS

The term 'pastry cutter' is uniquely British and refers to cutters that cut both pastry and biscuits. In continental Europe and North America pastry cutters are used for pastry, and biscuit or cookie cutters are used to cut out biscuit shapes.

Hand-carved wooden cutters have a long history in both North America and Europe. Early versions were known as imprint cutters because they imprinted a design on the dough. Having originated in Italy, they were used in Britain in the 15th century onwards to make gingerbread figures, often in the shape of popular contemporary personalities, such as Queen Elizabeth I or the first Lord Wellington. By the 18th century, they were used to make moulded sugar motifs to decorate cakes.

Later versions were outline cutters. These had a cutting edge, flat backs and usually a handle. Made from square or oblong-shaped wood, usually pear, walnut or beech, both types of wooden cutters were produced in Britain until the mid-19th century, when they were replaced by mass-produced metal ones.

◄ Tala produced a wide range of icing nozzles, related booklets and recipe ideas from the 1920s to the 1960s. Some icing sets incorporated a turntable to put the cake on while it was iced and which could be taken apart to be stored. The printed card (top) is the lid from a 1920s icing kit box

£5–15 a set

▼ This plastic turntable was made by Tala in the late 1950s and was available in several pastel colours. Always check the nozzles are original; these are are nickel-plated and date from pre-World War II. 1950s nozzles should be of stainless steel.

Turntable with box £12–15

ICING KITS

In the 19th century, forcing bags inserted with small pipes were used to make meringues or decorative mounds of creamed potatoes. The modern icing syringe, first introduced in the early 20th century, was a major improvement and came with a selection of screw-on nozzles which could make different patterns.

FLOUR DREDGERS & ROLLING PINS

▲ Quaker Oats produced this sugar shaker in the 1950s as a promotional item, but it could also be used for flour. Quaker Oats were founded by John Stuart who left Scotland in 1850 to open his first mill in Canada. The Quaker logo was chosen, as the purity of living and honesty of character of the Quaker movement were considered qualities needed to succeed.

£10–15

Flour is an essential ingredient in baking. Among the earliest flour utensils are rolling pins, which are known to have been used since the 17th century, originally hand-made from a variety of woods, such as sycamore, walnut, beech, fruitwood and ash. By the end of the 19th century, they were mass-produced and, in 1902, the firm Sears Roebuck, USA, introduced the revolving-handled rolling pin.

Different pins were made for different jobs: hollow glass pins were filled with crushed ice to keep pastry cool; ridged pins were used for crushing oats, salt or bread crumbs; and pie crust pins (which are tapered at the ends)

◄ This colourful flour dredger is made of porcelain. Produced in the 1950s (when polka dots were very popular), it is filled with flour from the base and has a special 'Suba Seal' stopper.

£7–10

► Made in the early 1900s, this tin flour sifter has an attractive porcelain knob on its rotary handle (they were more commonly made from wood). They were produced until the 1930s.

£15–20

were used to make the edge of the pie crust thicker than the middle.

Flour sifters and dredgers have been used for over 100 years and have changed little in design. Sifters are cups with a mesh across the base. The flour is sifted either by shaking or by turning a handle that moves revolving blades through the flour and allows it to pass through the sieve at the base. Flour dredgers work in a different way; shaped like canisters, they work when shaken upside down. They were mostly used for dusting flour on to a rolling pin or pastry board before rolling out pastry, but they could also be used to sprinkle sugar on to the top of pies or icing sugar on to cakes. Ceramic flour dredgers can make an attractive collection.

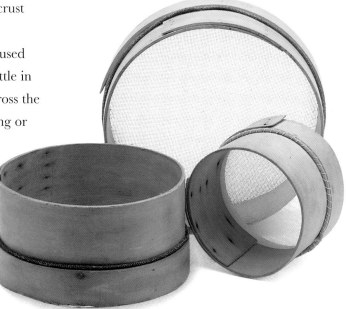

▲ Commonly known as cook's sieves or *tamis* (the French name for a drum sieve), sieves were available from the 1870s. Here, the earliest sieve (right) from the 1920s has a hair base; the large one from the 1930s to 1940s has a wire base, while the small sieve was made in the 1950s and has a nylon base.

£5–15 each

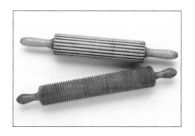

▲ These ridged pins were used for crushing oats. The bottom one was made in the 1860s – note how close and sharp the ridges are compared with the other, which was made in the 1930s. By this time, oats were more refined and so the pin has flatter ridges, more widely spaced apart.

Top: £25–30 | **Bottom: £50–65**

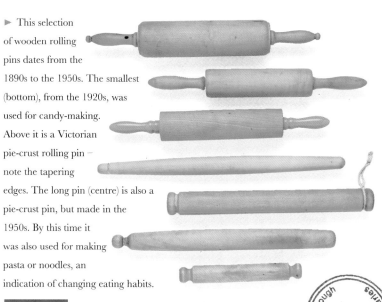

▶ This selection of wooden rolling pins dates from the 1890s to the 1950s. The smallest (bottom), from the 1920s, was used for candy-making. Above it is a Victorian pie-crust rolling pin – note the tapering edges. The long pin (centre) is also a pie-crust pin, but made in the 1950s. By this time it was also used for making pasta or noodles, an indication of changing eating habits.

£5–15 each

PIE PLATES & PIE FUNNELS

Pies as we know them were first made in the 18th century, using pastry that was moulded within a wooden or metal hoop which held it together while it baked. Some hoops had a strap handle to enable them to be lifted more easily. Later versions had metal hinges and these developed into tin and earthenware dishes and plates.

By the late 19th century, a wealth of different pie dishes were available. The traditional English pie dish was usually oval and deep enough to hold a filling. They had flat turned-out rims so that a pastry lid could be attached to the edge.

Pie funnels and cups are placed in the centre of a pie dish and poke up through the pastry, to support the crust and let out the steam from the filling at the same time.

▲ Although these enamel plates were originally sold as dinner plates, they were also well suited as pie plates. This alternative use was particularly popular in northern England, where they were used to bake shallow pies such as open tarts and mincemeat pies. Deeper enamel dishes were made specifically for baking pies and were available from an individual size up to a massive 16in (40cm.) version.

Production of enamel plates peaked from the 1930s to the 1950s. Cream plates with a green rim are generally from the 1930s, as are white ones with a black rim. Pale blue plates with a darker blue rim date from the 1930s to the 1940s, while white plates with a dark blue rim are from the 1950s.

Under £5 each

◄ These 1930s Pyrex shallow pie dishes have been well used – note the knife marks on the base – but, even so, have survived remarkably well. Pyrex is heat-resistant, making it a popular material for ovenware. These dishes were made from the 1930s to the 1940s and were available in varying sizes, from 7½in (19cm) to 11¾in (30cm).

Under £5 each

▶ T.G. Green & Co., best known as makers of Cornishware pottery, produced this unusual and elaborate individual pudding basin. It is stamped on the base 'Flamex ware' and 'T. G. Green Church Gresley Made in England', a mark used by the company from the 1920s to 1930s.

£8–12

▼ The large stoneware dish on the right dates from the 1920s and was used to make hotpot (a meat stew with potatoes) or Tattie pie (meat and potatoes with a shortcrust lid), both popular dishes in the north of England and Scotland. Made in the early 1900s, the shallow individual dish in the centre is made from creamware (a type of earthenware known as yellow ware in America). The individual dish on the left from the 1930s is made from earthenware which has been treacle-glazed.

£5 or under

▼ The three white funnels date from the 1920s to the 1940s. They are easy to find and, although plain in design, are all a little different in size and detail. The Patented Gourmet cup on the right was made in the 1900s and advertises the manufacturers' name. This one has a slight discolouration and small chips, but these are acceptable.

£5–15 each

▶ In North America, all pie funnels or cups are known as pie birds, whatever shape they are. However, this is the only true pie bird. It represents one of the four and twenty blackbirds that were, according to the English nursery rhyme, baked in a pie. Beware of reproductions, which are crudely modelled and coloured and are usually unmarked. The inside of original pie birds that were made in the 1930s, such as this one, are stamped 'Made in England' in green lettering.

£12–15

73

KITCHEN MOULDS

In the 19th century, moulds were commonly used in middle- and upper-class households, where cooks would prepare elaborate meals with either a savoury or a sweet jelly, blancmange or mousse as an impressive centrepiece. The most decorative moulds were made of copper and Wedgwood creamware, but they were also produced in white earthenware. By the turn of the 20th century, moulds were commercially made and were becoming available in a wider variety of materials.

A key figure in the history of moulds is Mrs. A.B. Marshall. A 19th-century English businesswoman, Mrs. Marshall, who was based in London, ran a cookery school and a domestic staff agency. She also sold speciality cooking ingredients, such as pistachio compound and liqueur syrups. She is best known for her *Illustrated Catalogue of Moulds and Special Kitchen Equipment*, published in 1886, in which she illustrates and describes over 1,000 moulds. The book may still be obtained today and is an essential reference work for the mould collector.

▼ Glass moulds were made in various shapes, such as tortoises (in the 1930 to 1940s) and rabbits and hares (1930s onwards). The glass mould impressed with the Star of David suggests it was produced for bar mitzvahs. The small mould was made in the 1920s, but is similar to a more decorative version available in the 1950s, sold with a ready-to-eat trifle.

£5–10 each

▼ These Victorian earthenware moulds would have been used to make a wide range of savoury dishes. Vegetables and fruits were often embossed on the base of the moulds to make attractive designs, such as asparagus (centre back) and cardoons (top right) – an unusual vegetable, similar to celery in appearance and a great delicacy in the 19th century. Embossed fruits included, most commonly, a pineapple – a sign of welcome – and at harvest time a wheatsheaf, signifying prosperity.

£20–45 each

► Following the invention of wire stands by E. Selman in 1931, manufacturers were able to produce moulds that could stand up, making them easier to pour liquid into. The large rabbit mould shown here and the swan were made in 1931 by Swan Brand. The small rabbit mould, for individual portions, was produced by the British firm Nutbrown, in the 1930s and again in the 1950s.

£5–15

▼ Beautifully made in a vast array of designs and sizes, copper moulds are the cream of all moulds, capable of producing sharply defined shapes. Their heyday was in the 19th century, from the 1830s onwards but even then they could be afforded only by the wealthy. During this time developments in close-plating and tinning safeguarded them against verdigris poisoning. Many copper moulds bear impressed names which relate almost always to the retailers rather than makers. Among the best-known retailers' marks found on copper moulds are Jones Bros., Ash Bros. & Heaton Ltd. and Benhams. These two moulds were produced from the 1860s to 1880; the one on the right is the rarer design.

Left: £120–150
Right: £150–180

► Production of JELL-O, a gelatine dessert, began in 1897 in North America and was introduced into Britain in the 1900s. In an attempt to promote the brand, these individual aluminium jelly moulds were made in the 1920s to the 1930s, stamped with the makers' name on the base. JELL-O was sold as jelly crystals and the booklet offers a selection of recipe ideas.

Book: £8–10 **Four mould set: £6–8**

▼ Cheese has traditionally been made in homemade wooden rings such as these from Normandy in France, for centuries. A cheese is wrapped in gauze or muslin, placed into the rings (available in different sizes) and left on a shelf to set and mature. New EC regulations on hygiene have banned their use in Europe, but they are still collectable for their decorative qualities.

£8–15 each

▲ Established in 1812, Joseph Bourne & Son are still among Britain's major producers of stoneware pottery. From 1912 to the 1930s they produced moulds in leadless glass stoneware – this one is from the 1920s. They also produced a range of kitchenware known as Denbyware.

£10–15

▼ Fish moulds are generally used to make mousse. These two are made from tin. The top one appears in Mrs. Marshall's book on moulds and was made in France in the 1870s. The other mould was first made in the 1930s and is still produced today – this one dates from the 1950s. Although attractive, it was made in such large numbers that it is not very valuable.

Top: £35–40   **Bottom: £8–12**

▲ Shortbread has long been associated with Scotland, although the original recipe is thought to have come from France. In Scotland it is traditionally eaten on New Year's Day, or Hogmanay (known as Cake Day). The shortbread mixture is pressed into hand-made wooden moulds, such as this one from c.1890 to produce a thin biscuit. More decorative ones were produced for tourists.

£35–45

▲ Presentation of food was extremely important to Victorians, who would impress their guests with spectacular displays at important dinner parties. This oval tin mould, made in the 1890s, would have been used to create a mousse border for dishes such as a seafood platter or a sweet mousse for a fruit dessert. Oval moulds are hard to come by so they are now highly desirable.

£10–15

▼ Although tin moulds are often thought of as the poor person's copper moulds, this example shows how attractive they could be. According to Mrs. Marshall's book, it was called a 'Solomon's Temple' (reflecting the 19th-century vogue for Ancient Egypt), and it would have been used to make a large multi-coloured savoury jelly.

£50–60

▼ This strange-shaped object would have been filled with a chicken mousse – the straps are there to stand the seamless mould on while filling it with the mixture. Made in France from 1870 to 1880, it has great curiosity value.

£45–60

▲ A large kugelhopf cake could be made in this mould. Kugelhopf is a rich bready cake with a yeasty dough which originated in Austria, but is also popular in France, Holland and Germany. The mould is hollow in the centre and the outer bowl is fluted and seamless so as not to spoil the pattern on the cake. This heavy tinned-steel German example from the 1920s was possibly used by a professional cook; domestic ones were also available. Kugelhopf moulds were also made in other materials, such as enamel, aluminium and earthenware.

£20–25

POTS & PANS

Boiling was the most simple and widely practised method of cooking until the 19th century, using large vessels known as cauldrons, kettles, boilers and crocks. Possibly the most well-known type of pot was the legged cauldron, which was usually made of bell metal, an alloy of copper and tin.

Although cauldrons were ideal for making large stews and soups, when smaller quantities were required skillets were used. These were pots with three short legs and very long handles, which were placed over a fire.

In the 18th century, with the introduction of the range (the first type of kitchen stove), skillets and cauldrons went into decline and were replaced by flat-bottomed saucepans, which rested on the hob, and pots which were placed inside the oven. In 1779, a Birmingham iron founder, John Izon, purchased the patent for making oval-bellied cast-iron pots which were tinned inside, making them lighter and cleaner. Further advances in technology led to the large-scale production of cooking pots, saucepans, stewpans and frying pans during the 18th and 19th century. Note that stewpans are straight sided, while saucepans are rounded. Curiously, boilers and saucepans have 'covers', but stewpans have tinned 'lids'.

By the 20th century, mass production meant pans were widely available; but some are still collectable.

▼ A Victorian earthenware colander.

EARLY COOKWARE

By 1800, saucepans made from cast iron were the most widely used and from 1840 onwards they were available with enamelled surfaces.

At the top end of the cookware range were graduating sets of heavy copper pans. Afforded only by the very wealthy who had a team of kitchen staff, these *batteries de cuisine* are highly sought after today. The sets would usually include at least one fish kettle, stew-pans and a bain-marie (for making sauces), as well as numerous different-sized saucepans.

Less expensive but still collectable are enamel, cast-iron and wrought-iron pans. Preserving pans were also widely produced. Usually made of brass, they are very attractive, but command high prices.

Other innovations of the 19th century included steamers, which allowed food to be cooked more gently, and double boilers, for cooking porridge.

In remote areas, such as parts of northern Britain and North America, traditional bakestones and griddles continued to be used well into the 20th century. Hand-forged examples are sought after today.

▼ Two types of fish kettle are shown here. On the left is a mackerel kettle, made from the 1900s to the 1930s. By the 1930s, handles were less heavy and made of tinned steel rather than iron. Before buying, be sure to check the drainer is not damaged and still has its lifting rings intact. The larger fish kettle from the 1920s (right) has a more domed lid than earlier ones and can also be used for boiling ham. Both differ from pre-1900 kettles which have flat lids.

Left: £30–35 **Right: £25–30**

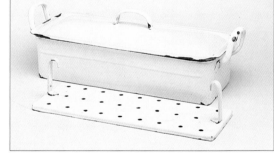

▲ Salmon kettles were devised for poaching a whole salmon. This Victorian example is made of vitreous enamelled iron, but they were also available in tinned steel or copper and, by the 1920s, aluminium. The perforated rack is used to lift and drain out the fish intact. Squarer-shaped fish kettles were made for poaching halibut, turbot or carp.

£35–45

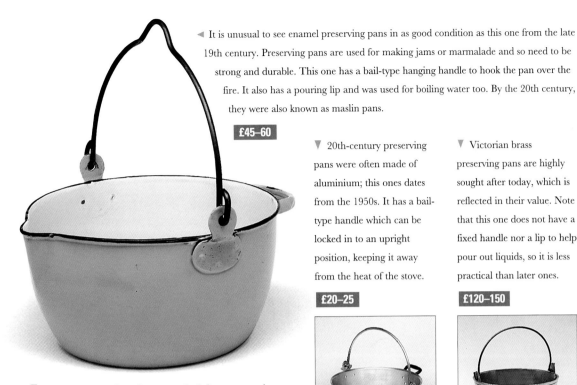

It is unusual to see enamel preserving pans in as good condition as this one from the late 19th century. Preserving pans are used for making jams or marmalade and so need to be strong and durable. This one has a bail-type hanging handle to hook the pan over the fire. It also has a pouring lip and was used for boiling water too. By the 20th century, they were also known as maslin pans.

£45–60

▼ 20th-century preserving pans were often made of aluminium; this ones dates from the 1950s. It has a bail-type handle which can be locked in to an upright position, keeping it away from the heat of the stove.

£20–25

▼ Victorian brass preserving pans are highly sought after today, which is reflected in their value. Note that this one does not have a fixed handle nor a lip to help pour out liquids, so it is less practical than later ones.

£120–150

▼ Meat griddles such as the one on the left are extremely rare today. Made in the 18th century, the iron bars along the base originally allowed the fat of the meat to drip through on to the fire, which would cause the flames to shoot up and char the meat. The other pan is a 19th-century hanging frying pan. Fairly deep, it was ideal for broiling or stewing.

Left: £60–75 **Right: £25–35**

► Both these griddles are Scottish and were made in the 19th century. The one on the right has a clip that holds the handle rigid when cooking. The other griddle has a fixed handle, which is less desirable.

Left: £20–25 **Right: £25–30**

GRIDDLES
Griddles developed from simple bakestones, first used in Roman times. Bakestones were originally made of sandstone, which developed into flat sheets of iron and became known as griddles. Used for cooking oatcakes, pancakes or meat, griddles were suspended over a fire by a strong semi-circular handle. 18th- and 19th-century griddles are mostly found in rural areas today.

LATER COOKWARE

By 1900, saucepans were mass-produced and easily affordable by most households. Electric and gas stoves made cooking less messy (open-fire ranges left a residue of smoke and dirt on pans) and the cleaning of pans became an important consideration, especially as the current wisdom of the day insisted that the bottom of a pan should be as clean as the inside. Previously, it was thought that pans cooked better with some build-up on the base and sides.

Aluminium pans were also available, but it is advisable not to use them for cooking unless they were made after 1920. By this time, most aluminium saucepans made in Britain bore the guarantee of the makers that they were between 98 and 99 per cent pure.

Copper pans were phased out in the early 20th century. They were costly and time-consuming to produce, expensive to buy and impractical for the modern kitchen.

▲ The mottled enamel of this Dutch milk pan (left) is often wrongly mistaken for American graniteware. With careful examination a difference can be seen – American enamel does not have any black in the mottling. The special feature of this pan, which was made in the 1950s, is its sharp pouring lip.

Part of a larger range, the shaded orange enamel pan was made in France in the 1930s. A similar set was produced in the 1950s, but with a bluish/grey interior.

Left: £6–9   **Right: £7–10**

▼ The early 1950s-style pale green enamel saucepan (left) carries the Jury brand name. In excellent condition, it is made of an unusual combination of materials: a cast-iron base (which makes the pan heavy), an enamelled body and an aluminium lid with a heat-resisting handle and lid knob.

Crown Merton produced aluminium hollow ware (pots and pans) from the late 1920s to the 1950s. The lipped pan (right) from the 1930s was designed to be used on the hotplates of electric ovens and came with its own lid. Great care has been taken with the design, and both the handle and lid knob are insulated with heat-resisting Bakelite.

Left: £15–20   **Right: £12–15**

▶ The square saucepan was first made in the late 1920s and was especially recommended for electric hotplates as a space saver, This set has the Daleware trademark and all the pans have pouring lips. The stove enamel pan (right) was patented and manufactured by Siddons Ltd. from 1932 onwards.

Left: £30–40 **Right: £28–36**

◀ Most frying pans were made from wrought iron, although cast iron and copper were used too. This selection of pans from the 1890s-1920s includes an enamelled steel pan (left) from the 1920s specially made for use on a cooker range with a hob. The base was stepped to fit into the hob, so the bottom of the pan was not in contact with the fire. The smallest pan (right) is a French oval skillet made from 1910 to the 1920s. Pans such as these are very rare.

£6–35

▼ These three pans from the 1920s to the 1950s were made by Judge Brand. The boiler (centre) holds up to 2 gallons (or 9 litres), while the garish blue colour of the saucepan (left), when combined with black enamel, suggests it was made in the 1950s. The stewpan on the right is from the 1930s.

Left: £7–10 **Centre: £30–35** **Right: £12–16**

▲ Although the two stands shown here do not belong to these particular tins, they would have stood in a similar roasting tin or a large pan to allow the fat from a joint of meat to drip through into the pan while the meat cooked. On the left is an American graniteware roasting tin made from 1900 to the 1920s. To its right is a tinned-steel roasting tin from the 1920s.

Left tin: £14–18 **Right tin: £6–8** **Stands: £4–8**

TRIVETS & SAUCEPAN STANDS

▲ The dragon on this pot stand from the 19th century is typical of the Chinese influence found in many earthenware items of this period.

£40–50

Before the 1800s, trivets, for standing a kettle or pan on, were very simple, made from wrought iron and twisted into shapes. Various kinds were made, including one with long legs that was placed in the fire and acted as a stand for the pot during cooking. In the 19th century the Pennsylvania Dutch produced iron trivets, often made into decorative heart shapes.

With the development of the kitchen range in the 18th century, trivets were made that hooked on to the front of the grate of a stove

▲ Not all trivets were elaborately made. This simple 19th-century wooden example is from Scotland and would have been made at home, carved from a single piece of wood. It has three bun feet and a hole in one corner to hang it near the range. It is rare to find a wooden trivet, so this one is very sought after. Note the way the wood has aged over the years and charred in places from hot pans, all of which adds greatly to its appeal.

£25–30

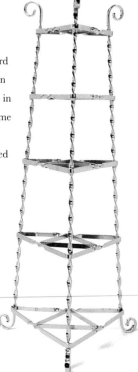

▶ It is unusual to find a saucepan stand that has been chrome-plated (chrome is a hard metal used to increase corrosion resistance). This one was made in the 1930s, a period when chrome was very popular, and it was probably specially commissioned for a modern kitchen.

On the right is a 1930s hand-forged saucepan stand. Unusually, it has only three tiers (four or five were more common), making it unpractical for all but the smallest households.

£15–40 each

and were used to keep pots warm. Among the most elaborately designed trivets were 'footmen' which were kept in the sitting-room as a stand for a tea kettle or a plate of muffins or crumpets. Less decorative versions would have been found in the kitchen and used by the servants.

Similar to trivets were brandreths, which were used for holding bakestones, griddles and pans close to the fire for cooking. They were still widely used until the early 20th century in remote areas of Scotland and Wales.

Pan stands were made in all types of metal strong enough to support the weight of up to seven pans from the 19th century onwards.

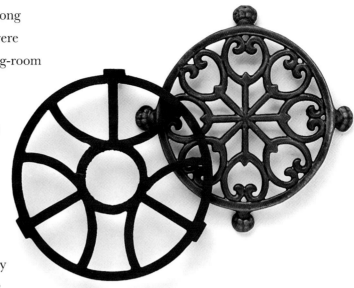

▲ The item on the left is a simple 1900s iron stand used to place the pot on from the stove. The other is a recast Victorian trivet from the 1930s of vitreous pearlized enamel.

Left: £7–10   **Right: £12–16**

► The most distinctive features of the 1920s iron hearth stand on the left made by Spong are its japanned legs, which are extendable. Made in the 1950s, the pressed steel trivet (right) is more flimsy.

£6–16

SAUCEPAN STANDS

Saucepan stands were first made for use in the kitchen of large houses in the 19th century to store a column of gleaming pans. Early stands were often very large – with up to 14 tiers – but by the early 20th century they were smaller, averaging five to seven tiers. Most stands were made from black japanned iron, although painted stands could be specially ordered if required. Alternatively, small tins of paint were available to paint stands at home – this would be less expensive.

STEAMERS & PANS

Cooking by steam was first practised in the 1840s, when double saucepans (made of iron) were introduced for making sauces and custards in wealthy homes. However, it was not until the development of the Captain Warren cooking pot in the 1870s that steaming was adopted on a large scale. Named after its inventor, the 'Captain Warren cooking pot' was a large oval tinned-steel pan with a tight-fitting lid, consisting of three interlocking compartments connected by a tube which allowed steam in to cook the food.

A heavy steamer saucepan with a porcelain inner pan and a wooden handle attached to a collar around the inner pan's top was introduced in the 1870s which became very popular in North America. By the late 19th century, porringers, also known as double boilers, were available.

Another ingenious device, the egg poacher, was originally known as a steamer in Britain, but as a poacher in North America. The covered pan poacher was developed in Britain by c.1900 and has remained unchanged.

▲ This large tinned-steel sterilizer is an unusual implement and works in a similar way to a steamer. Water is placed at the bottom part and the steam rises up through the holes in the base to cook the food above. The separate round piece to its right fits inside to form a shelf for puddings or joints of meat. This one was made in the late 19th century.

£20–35

▼ The top of the large tin steamer (right) has a stepped bottom, allowing it to fit different sized pans, advertised as a 'Universal Fitting'. Available from the 1900s to the 1930s, it was called the 'A.B.C.'.

The grey-mottled enamel steamer (left) is Dutch and was made from the 1920s to the 1930s. This example would be much more valuable if it had its original base, although it could still be used on a saucepan of the correct-fitting size.

Left: £14–18   **Right: £18–24**

▲ Enamel porringers, or double boilers, were made by a number of manufacturers. This one (left), from the 1930s, has the Judge Brand trademark and could also be used to cook porridge or to make sauces as it eliminated the chance of burning. Porringers were often made in aluminium by the 1930s, pre-1930s ones have tinned steel handles, such as this one.

Left: £15–18   Right: £6–10

▶ Known as a steamer tower, this aluminium pan was available in two and three tiers and carries the Swan Brand trademark. Made from the late 1920s to the 1930s, it features a lifting rack.

£16–25

▲ This rare porringer is called the 'Quaker Oats Cooker': offered by Quaker from the 1890s to 1920 in return for Quaker Oats box lids, was an excellent way of promoting their brand. This one was made in North America, although they were also exported to Europe. Note the blue lettering, 'Quaker Oats Cooker', around the top collar of the pan, which makes it particularly valuable.

To make porridge with a porringer, water is put into the bottom part of the pan. Oats and water are put into the top section which fits into the base and are brought slowly to the boil and then simmered, stirring occasionally.

£100–125

▶ This selection of egg poachers dates from the 1890s to the 1940s. The earliest is the rare blue-mottled vitreous enamel two-cup egg poacher (centre), made in North America in the 1890s. Equally rare is the Edwardian aluminium four-cup poacher (left). It is unusual to find a poacher of this age still complete with all its cups and in such good condition.

£10–25 each

◀ Tinned-steel colanders, as shown here, were popular in the late 19th century. However, the one on the right has acquired a lovely patina over the years, suggesting it was well-used and hung up in a kitchen rather than stored away. The one on the left, although similar, was made in the 1920s and has noticeably thinner handles.

Left: £20–25 **Right:£30–35**

COLANDERS, STRAINERS & DRAINERS

Although a colander is used to drain food cooked in liquid, confusingly the name is derived from the Latin, *colare*, to strain. Their basic design has not changed greatly since Ancient Egyptian times, comprising a bowl with perforated holes in the base and side with two handles. Colanders with a ring base, feet or peg-legs are known as 'foot-fast', while those without such a base are commonly known as 'foot-loose'. 18th-century colanders were often made from brass or even copper, but by the 19th century, tin, earthenware, enamel and copper were also used.

Strainers and drainers have different functions: a drainer has larger perforations and is used to drain water away from food, while a strainer strains the food through a mesh leaving the unwanted lumps behind.

▲ Bearing the Falconware trademark, this aluminium colander (left) made from the 1920s to the 1930s is both attractive and practical. Check the legs are still firm; with constant use they can work loose and cannot be tightened. The 1940s Corfalgar colander (right) was made by Crown Merton.

Left: £8–15 **Right: £7–10**

▼ Made in France in the 1920s, this unusual and rare piece is a fish drainer. The fish is washed and prepared and laid in the basket to drain away any excess water. Occasionally this item is mistaken for a plate drainer.

£45–55

▼ Enamel has been a popular material for making colanders since the 1900s in Britain, while in North America it has been used since the 1880s. The cream foot-fast colander with a pale blue trim was made in the 1950s. It has been more lightly enamelled than earlier examples, a characteristic of this period. It is still collectable, however, as it is in very good condition with only a few exterior chips.

Behind it is an example of early North American graniteware. The colander is in the form of a pan, with a long handle and even a strap support for resting the pan. Made c.1900, the enamel has been applied on to iron, making it heavy, but durable.

A most unusual example is the small pan colander (bottom left), from Finland. This country had a thriving enamel industry until World War II. The aqua-green colour of the handle and rim appear to be unique to Finnish enamelware.

£8–25 each

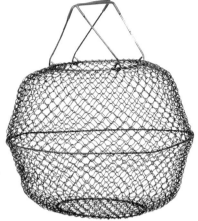

▲ This French salad shaker was made in the 1930s. Although salad shakers and drainers are both used to drain excess water away from lettuce, shakers are made of flexible wire netting, while salad baskets are usually made of stronger wire. France is one of the main centres of production of both types.

£15–20

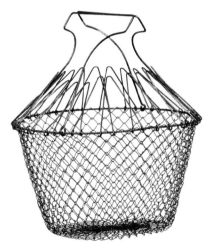

▲ Salad shakers are simple to store as the flexible netting easily collapses. This one was made in France in the early 1900s, although the design is still used.

£12–16

► Made in the 19th century, this French wire salad basket has been beautifully produced. The top section closes together snugly and the wire has been carefully twisted around the frame. Condition is often a problem with wire salad baskets as they spend so much time being wet and can become very rusty. However, this one is in remarkably good condition with only superficial rust, which is reflected in its value.

Although similar to egg baskets, baskets for shaking salad have much smaller openings. Some have a piece of looped wire attached that can be folded over the opening when shaking the salad.

£45–60

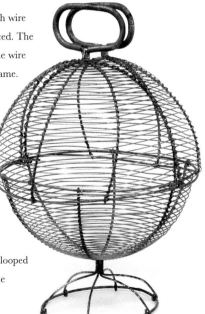

WAFFLE IRONS & OTHER ITEMS

Waffle irons originated in Europe in the 18th century. They developed from wafer irons which date back to the 15th century and were originally used to make wafers for Christian Communion services. Wafer irons are much rarer than waffle irons and are highly sought after today.

Wafer irons are distinguished from waffle irons by their round shape and smaller size. Early versions were made of very heavy cast iron and were similar in design to a pair of tongs. At the end of two long arms are hinged plates (either round or square), plain on the outside and patterned inside.

These patterns varied greatly from maker to maker, but the most common were grids of geometric shapes, such as squares, circles and diamonds. By the late 19th century, waffle irons had developed into a rectangular or square shape, in the form of a hinged iron box, with a raised pattern on the inside of the base and lid.

By the 1930s, heavy chromium plate waffle makers were produced, which are similar to those manufactured today. Look out for variations too, such as fritter makers. Packaging is always a bonus too.

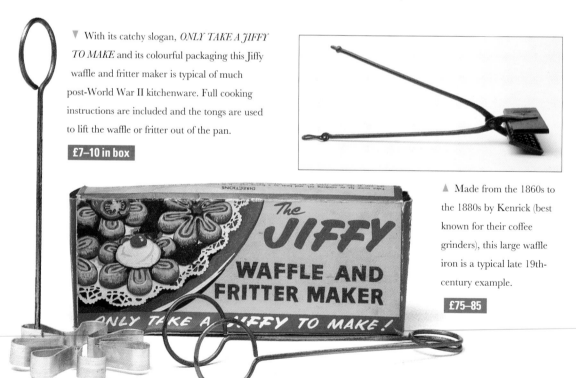

▼ With its catchy slogan, *ONLY TAKE A JIFFY TO MAKE* and its colourful packaging this Jiffy waffle and fritter maker is typical of much post-World War II kitchenware. Full cooking instructions are included and the tongs are used to lift the waffle or fritter out of the pan.

£7–10 in box

▲ Made from the 1860s to the 1880s by Kenrick (best known for their coffee grinders), this large waffle iron is a typical late 19th-century example.

£75–85

◀ Used to protect meat and other food from flies, covers made from wire or muslin were produced from the late 1870s until the 1950s. 19th-century covers, such as this one, with attractive elaborate handles, are the most sought after, although muslin-covered meat safes used for protecting a large piece of meat are also collectable. Small muslin covers can be attractive too. Used to cover milk jugs, they were decorated with coloured beads to weigh them down and to prevent them slipping off.

£12–16

▼ When ovens and stoves were first mass-produced, from 1910 onwards, manufacturers usually included cooking guidelines. This one is in excellent condition and can be read easily.

£10–15

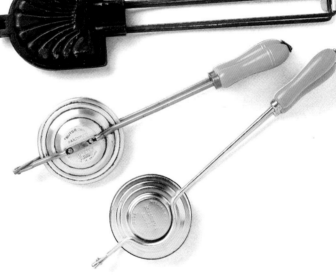

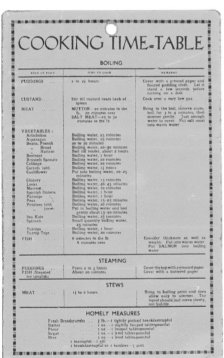

COOKING TIME-TABLE

BOILING

▲ Sandwich toasters developed from waffle irons and work on the same principle. The two toasters (centre and bottom) were made in the 1950s. The one with the green handle was made by Nutbrown. The blue-handled 'Rite Tasti' toaster (bottom), by Made Rite is not of such high quality as the Nutbrown version and would have been less expensive. At the top of the picture is a cast-aluminium waffle iron. This example is embossed which means it was made after 1900; pre-1900 they were made with flat tops.

£5–20 each

CHOPPING & GRINDING

Chopping and grinding were carried out with the same type of equipment for centuries, and there was little progress in the development of mechanical kitchen implements until after the Great Exhibition of 1851. The success of this enormous showcase for industrial Britain spurred makers into inventing a whole range of new implements and gadgets, which were launched at further trade fairs. After one such exhibition, in 1854, *The Times* newspaper in London praised the 'ingenious mincing machine' exhibited by Nye & Company of Soho, London, which could make an impressive 8lb (3.6kg) of minced meat in four minutes.

By the 1860s, mincers, sausage-making machines, apple corers and peelers were available and other labour-saving devices, such as mechanical choppers, bean slicers, raisin stoners, potato mashers and rotary graters quickly followed.

Most items were made of cast iron until the late 19th century, when steel and, later, stainless steel became more usual.

▼ A 1910 French pepper mill with silver plate bands.

HERB & SPICE CHOPPERS

In the early 18th century, with swords no longer in great demand, swordsmiths turned their skills to making knives and gardening tools. The blades of choppers were usually crescent-shaped and 'pierced' with attractive designs, such as doves and flowers.

The Industrial Revolution in the 18th century meant the design of large tools, such as spades and hoes, underwent a great improvement which, in turn, led to better-quality utensils and cutlery in the kitchen.

By the 19th century, domestic chopping equipment was made on a large scale in Britain in industrialized tool-making centres such as Sheffield in Yorkshire. In continental Europe and North America, however, it was more usual for tools such as choppers still to be made by local craftsmen. As a result, it is difficult to identify the makers of many choppers as they are usually unmarked.

In all countries, blades were originally made of iron, then fine steel in the 19th century and stainless steel from the 1930s onwards.

It is worth noting that flat metal herb and spice choppers are traditionally used on chopping boards, and those with curved blades are for wooden bowls or mortars.

HERBS & SPICES IN COOKERY

In the 17th century, when spices were still a novelty in the West, the word was applied to sugary as well as spicy items. The distinction lay between *épices de chambre*, which included fennel and marzipan, and *épices de cuisine*. The latter group covered products no longer considered as spices, such as milk and honey, as well as others which have totally disappeared, such as musk and amber. In cooking, generous amounts of spice were added to disguise the foul taste of tainted meat or to add flavour to the bland food eaten by the poor.

By the 19th century, spices had established different purposes and were used judiciously. They were kept in attractive storage jars (see p.20) and ground with choppers and mortars and pestles when needed.

Herbs are used in cooking in a slightly different way from spices. They have a less strong taste and are useful for adding an aromatic flavour or as a garnish. It is worth remembering that until the 17th century, the word 'herb' encompassed all types of plant, and choppers and grinders would have been used to cut plants used in medicine, food and drinks.

▲ Made from the late 1930s to the 1940s, this chopper carries the Skyline trademark and comprises three blades. The centre blade is slightly longer than the other two and is connected to a coiled spring so they can chop together.

£10–14

An international selection of herb choppers is illustrated here. The earliest (bottom), a typical American design of this period, was made in North America in the mid-19th century. The style of the handle is known as a 'tiller' handle, while the feral (the part that joins the blade and handle) is made from brass.

Top left is an English chopper with a tee-shaped handle stamped 'Sheffield' on the blade. This one was made in the early 1900s, although identical ones were still available in the 1930s. The other one was made in France in the 1950s and has a 'rocker-style' blade, which has been stamped with the makers' name, Rival.

£16–45

The turned fruitwood handle on this chopping knife is very unusual and adds significantly to its value. Made in England in the 19th century, this chopper is unmarked and its manufacturer is unknown.

£25–35

A rare 18th-century example, this French chopping knife has an unusual 'tiller' style wooden handle and the blade is made of wrought iron. This design continued into the 19th century and was found both in Europe and North America. This type of chopper is particularly sought after by collectors.

£50–70

95

▶ This gadget was made in North America c.1880 to 1900 for grating nutmeg. Stored in the handle, the nutmeg fits into the mechanism and is ground by turning the handle. There is a wire brush for cleaning the grater.

£50–70

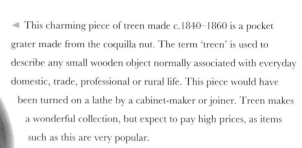

◀ This charming piece of treen made c.1840–1860 is a pocket grater made from the coquilla nut. The term 'treen' is used to describe any small wooden object normally associated with everyday domestic, trade, professional or rural life. This piece would have been turned on a lathe by a cabinet-maker or joiner. Treen makes a wonderful collection, but expect to pay high prices, as items such as this are very popular.

The nutmeg would have been kept inside the acorn along with the grater. The metal grater is encircled by a piece of ivory and this is screwed into the wood. Beware, the ivory is often cracked and the grater is prone to rust.

£90–120

▶ This nutmeg grater made from 1870 to 1890 would have been carried around by a gentleman in his jacket pocket and used to grate nutmeg on to drinks such as mulled wine, milk or hot chocolate. A compact shape, the grater opens up for grating, and folds neatly back when not in use.

Originally this attractive grater would have been japanned, but the colour has gradually worn off over the years, as often happens. As a result, the value has been slightly lowered.

£40–50

PESTLES & MORTARS

The pestle and mortar was used for a variety of purposes in the kitchen, including pounding herbs and spices, crushing salt and mashing vegetables. It was also used by apothecaries, who specialized in making medicines from herbs and spices; as well as in coffee houses for grinding coffee, and in tobacco shops, where tobacco was crushed into snuff.

The various shapes of the mortar – cylindrical, hexagonal and octagonal – date back to the 17th century and they were made in all sizes from a few inches/centimetres high to massive floor-standing ones up to 5ft (1.5m) high. Floor-standing mortars were usually made of stone or marble, while wood was used for smaller ones. Oak, elm, beech and walnut were common, but the favourite was lignum vitae, partly because it was supposed to have medicinal qualities.

By the 19th century, Wedgwood were the best-known makers of earthenware mortars and pestles and many have survived today.

▲ Kenrick (best-known for their coffee grinders) made cast-iron pestles and mortars in different sizes between 1860 and 1900. Marked on the base, this one is the smallest, a ¼ pint (0.15 litre) size.

£75–90

▲ This wooden mortar dates back from the late 18th century and it is remarkable that it has survived. A very rare item, it is still in excellent condition, with traces of the original red paint still visible on the outside.

£150–200

▼ Various materials have been used to make mortars, but among the most hard-wearing is marble. The larger one (below) dates from 1800, while the smaller is stamped 'Made in England', dating it after 1900. Major makers include Wedgwood, which produced them in earthenware.

Left: £40–60   **Right: £35–45**

MINCERS & SLICERS

One of the most popular types of slicers with collectors are marmalade cutters, which are to Britain what apple parers are to North America (see p.108). First produced in the late 19th century, early marmalade cutters typically comprised a heavy iron mechanism that clamped on to a table and worked with a lever action. The 'Universal' marmalade cutter from 1900 is typical: the fruit was fed through a hopper (a type of funnel) and pushed down with a wooden pestle. The oranges were then chopped by a blade attached to a heavy lever that was worked to and fro by hand.

By the 1920s, new designs were introduced, such as a novel orange shredder shaped like a patty pan. Made of tinned steel, it had cutting perforations and the orange was worked by hand around the shredder. Sadly, although ingenious, it was not as efficient or fast as other slicers and few were produced.

Mincers first appeared in the 1870s for the grinding and mincing of meat and were generally made from tinned steel, cast iron and enamelled iron or tin. Among the main makers of mincers in Britain were Spong, which produced a wide variety of machines for domestic and professional catering use, all with the same basic operations. In North America, mincers were known as grinders and first appeared in large numbers from the 1890s. Well-known makers include the Enterprise Manufacturing Company.

◄ An unusual combination of materials has been used to make this 1950s Spong mincer (left) – the base is made of green enamel on aluminium, the top part and handle arm are steel and it has a wooden handle. In the centre is a plain green enamel mincer. Although the makers are unknown, it is still collectable and has four assorted cutting discs. Made in the 1930s, the largest mincer (right) was produced by the British firm, Harpers. An unusual feature is an Australian patent as well as a British one, which adds both interest and value to the piece.

£10–16

◀ These three bean slicers date from the 1930s to the 1950s. The earliest (centre) is embossed 'Spong's Bean Slicer' No. 632' around the front disc. This slicer has two hoppers so it could accommodate different sizes of beans and consists of two parts, the outer casing and the inner casing, which held three detachable blades. In the 1950s Spong produced the light-painted aluminium slicer (left). It also has three blades, but they have been fixed into the inner disc, making them difficult to sharpen. Also of aluminium, the other slicer (right) was produced by unknown Dutch makers in the 1950s. Almost aerodynamic in design, it is an unusual piece and would make a worthwhile addition to a collection.

£6–18 each

▼ Although produced as a marmalade slicer in the 1930s, this Spong's slicer was promoted as a general-purpose slicer for carrots, potatoes and other vegetables, so appealing to a greater number of buyers. It has an acid-proof brown lacquer finish for durability.

£14–18

▶ This is a rotary marmalade machine, used for slicing orange peel. It carries the 'Rapid' brand name (printed around the front disc in raised letters) and was made in the 1920s. This type of rotary cutter works by feeding oranges through a hopper at the back and then pressing them through with a pestle. Note it has to be clamped on to the table.

£20–25

BEAN SLICERS

Bean slicers appear to be peculiar to Europe. In Britain very ornate japanned cast-iron bean slicers were produced in the late 19th century. The beans were fed down a hopper and the slicer cleverly topped, tailed, edged and finally sliced the bean between cutter blades. Similar slicers were produced throughout Europe. Look out for late 19th-century German ones, which can be identified as they carry an embossed trademark of a hand.

MASHERS & CHOPPERS

Since Elizabethan times, simple heavy 'hammers' were used for beating meat and fish. With the introduction of potatoes, wooden potato mashers were developed and these remained similar in shape until the 1890s. Variations developed too, such as potato ricers and chippers.

Other types of masher available from the 19th century onwards included a spinach press, a cabbage press and special mashers for soft fruit.

▼ Made of heavy cast iron, the potato ricer, a device for preparing potatoes, evolved in the 1890s. Cooked potatoes are put into a perforated container and the handle pressed, which makes the potatoes ooze out like small grains of rice. By the 20th century, many different potato ricers were produced by numerous companies, such as tinned-steel ricers and a tinned-iron one called the 'O.K.' in the 1920s and 1930s. The one on the left was made by Kenrick & Sons in the 1900s, while the other, dating from the 1940s was produced by Tala.

Left: £14–18 **Right: £10–14**

▼ According to its makers the Rotary Company, with this gadget 'one clean quick stroke produces two dozen chips'. Originally patented in the 1930s, this potato chipper was produced in the 1950s. The attractive packaging, typical of the period, adds significantly to its value.

£10–14

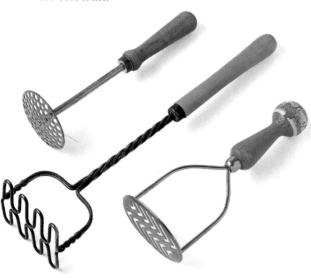

▲ On the left is a spinach press made in the 1930s by Tala – distinguished from a potato masher by the single rod. In the centre is a 1920s potato masher. The green wooden handle with the ivory band of the Skyline masher (right) helps identify that it was made in the 1930s.

Left: £8–12 **Centre: £12–15** **Right: £5 or under**

► This large mushroom-shaped press dates from the 19th century and would have been used to press soft cooked fruits or vegetables such as cabbage through a cook's sieve. Made of smooth golden wood, it is a tool that has been well-used.

£20–24

▼ 20th-century choppers for vegetables came in many different forms and were used to chop up cooked vegetables, as well to give a crinkled edge to raw vegetables. On the bottom right is an early 1900s vegetable chopper of corrugated tin, while above is a red-handled stainless steel chopper from the late 1950s to early 1960s, which carries the Skyline trademark. Potato chippers (also used as vegetable dicers) were popular too. The one shown here (left) was made in the 1930s by Tala.

£5–8 each

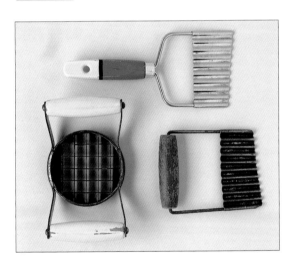

► On the left is an early 19th-century Irish potato masher. It is very simple and primitive-looking, but note the slight decoration on the handle, which gives a firm grip. This type of masher is very collectable, as are all early wooden pieces.

Early Victorian mashers, such as the one shown here (right), also known as beetles, are sought after too. Made from one solid piece of wood, it would have been used for mashing all types of food, from potatoes to fish.

Left: £25–30 **Right: £30–40**

101

GRATERS & SLICERS

Punched iron graters have been used in cooking for centuries, mainly for grating hard cheese or breadcrumbs from stale bread. Sheet brass graters were introduced into Britain when Dutch brass workers arrived in the 16th century and they even warranted a mention in Samuel Pepys' diaries in the 17th century.

However, graters were most commonly used in cooking and were found in a wide variety of shapes and sizes. Early 19th-century tinplate graters comprised sheets of punched metal with rolled edges around an iron or wire frame; later, the joins were machine-pressed or seamed.

▲ On the left is a small bread rasp which was available in three sizes; their main purpose was to scrape the burnt bottoms of loaves. Graters sometimes came with a special wooden box to catch the gratings. However, the box in the centre is not original, which reduces the value of this c.1900 grater. On the right is an unusual lightweight aluminium slicer with a foldaway wire stand made in the 1950s for slicing vegetables.

Left: £5–7 **Centre: £8–12** **Right: Under £5**

▶ Victorian graters such as this one (left) by Acme, are very collectable. The homemade grater on the right was also made in the 19th century and is known as a 'primitive' collectable.

£8–16 each

◀ These three graters are made of tin. Known as the 'Cook's Indispensable', the grater on the left, made from the 1920s to 1930,s can be used for grating and slicing. In the centre is a round patterned grater with a strap handle, which has three surfaces – fine, medium and coarse – which was made from the 1920s to the 1930s. On the right is an square-shaped grater, 'The Premier', made from the 1900s to the 1930s.

£6–14 each

▼ It is rare to find kitchen utensils still with their original packaging, and even rarer to find they have never been used. Made in the 1950s, this peeler, shredder and slicer is in excellent condition. Note Nutbrown's assertion that it is suitable for 'right and left handed people' – an unusual selling point, but very practical.

£5–8

▶ An ingenious gadget, this is a coconut grater; its very sharp serrated blades are used to shred the inside of the coconut. Possibly made in the mid-19th century for use in British colonies, it is a very rare piece and would be highly sought after by collectors.

£35–45

◀ Made from the late 1940s to the early 1950s, this colourful tomato slicer with its original packaging sleeve has survived in excellent condition. Ideal for slicing firm tomatoes, it was made in Britain, it carries the Skyline brand name.

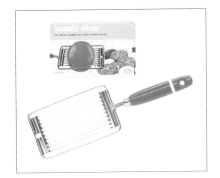

£6–8 (with packaging)

▶ Although this 19th-century slicer looks similar to a cucumber slicer, it was used for making sauerkraut (a vegetable dish of sliced cabbage). Note the large screw on the end, used to adjust the thickness of the steel blade. Slicers such as these were very common in continental Europe and the design has never greatly changed.

£45–60

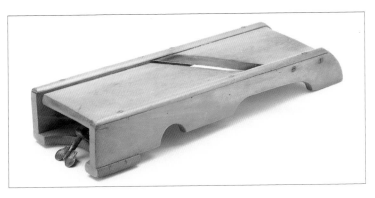

◀ The cucumber slicer on the right dates from the 1860s and has a steel blade which can be taken out for cleaning and sharpening. On the left is a slicer made in the 1920s.

Left: £10–15   Right: £25–35

▲ Note the hanging ring on the 1920s butcher's steel (top). This was to enable the butcher to hang it from his waist and so have it to hand at all times. This example also has a finger guard to help prevent the knife from sliding up. Below is a late Victorian cook's steel. Note how much smaller it is than the butcher's steel, indicating it was for domestic use.

Top: £12–16 **Bottom: £10–15**

▼ Large meat choppers, or cleavers, consist of a blade on a wooden handle, usually of beech, ash, sycamore or fruitwood and were used both for chopping meat and disjointing bones. By the 19th century, choppers were mostly made in Sheffield, home of the British steel industry, and therefore many are stamped 'Sheffield Steel' on the blade. Top is a mid-Victorian meat cleaver; below it is a French meat cleaver from the 1900s. It is distinguished by its typical French shape – note the way the blade turns up at the end.

£20–25 each

MEAT UTENSILS & SHARPENERS

Kitchen knives have been among the cook's most important tools for many centuries. Expensive to produce, they were made to last a long time. The very earliest knives were carved from a piece of stone or bone, but by the Iron Age, developments in metal-working meant iron was used.

By the 19th century, knives were made of steel too and, from the 1920s, were mass-produced in stainless steel. Until then, knives had always been hand-forged and were prone to rusting. Knife sharpening was traditionally carried out by knife grinders who would

travel the country sharpening knives on a large stone. 'Steels' were the first type of domestic sharpener to be widely used and date from the mid-19th century.

All steels are the same basic long heavy shape, often differing only in the type of handle used; some had horn handles, others wooden handles.

Knife sharpeners as we know them date from the 20th century. Although produced in different shapes and sizes, they all work on the same principle: by drawing the knife blade back and forth over the gap between the discs, the knife is sharpened.

▼ It is unusual to find a meat tenderizer in such good condition. This one was made in the 1930s, one end is formed from a piece of dented aluminium, the other side is smooth wood. The overall design has not changed, although later ones have steel end pieces.

£6–10

◄ This 1920s French meat hook would have slipped on to a rod hanging in a butcher's refrigerator with half an animal carcass on either side. In Britain, a whole carcass is traditionally hung on one hook.

Today, these strong hooks can be used to hang kitchen utensils such as small wirework storage baskets.

£15–20

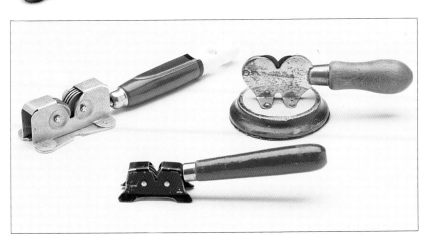

◄ The oldest sharpener here is the 'heart-shaped' one made from 1910 to 1920. On the left is a Skyline knife sharpener from the late 1950s. First introduced in the 1930s, it was copied by many makers. The other sharpener is a slim version of this design by an unknown maker of the 1930s.

£5–12 each

BREADBOARDS & KNIVES

Judging the age of wooden items can be difficult, unless one knows the clues to look for. With breadboards, early examples tend to have a worn appearance after years of use for bread cutting. Check the condition of the board carefully, and avoid those with a dry white look, as these will have been immersed in water for long periods and be prone to warping. To prolong the life of a wooden board, when cleaning it simply wipe it over with a damp cloth to remove any crumbs or stickiness.

Bread knives are highly collectable too, particularly those made in the 19th and early 20th century which have been carved with the name of a bakery – Allinson, Hovis and Turog are among the best known. Other collectable bread knives include those carved with the word 'bread', and those made by ex-servicemen in the late 1940s. These are etched on the blade: 'This knife has been made by genuine ex-servicemen'; they received a percentage of the sales.

Wavy serrated knives date from the early 1890s. A more jagged serrated blade was produced in the early 1930s. Handles were made from metal, Bakelite, Xylonite (a type of plastic) or bone in a wide range of shapes.

▲ Although there is some wear and tear on this breadboard, it is an attractive piece and worth collecting. Made of English sycamore, it has been carefully carved with ears of wheat and the word 'Welcome'. The style of carving on breadboards varied over the years: Victorian boards can be distinguished by fancy lettering, whereas, from the 1920s onwards, lettering became plainer. Some carving was done by manufacturers, although it was also commonly added at home.

£20–25

THE CUTTING EDGE

'Bread knives are made in a large variety of different sizes and shapes. It is best to spend more than a few pennies on such a tool, but there again there is no need to spend very much. A good bread knife saves a great deal of time and bread. The edge should be considered carefully.

'One which is finely serrated, with the serration going in alternate directions every few inches up the blade, is particularly good. This makes less crumbs when the bread is new.'

From *Easier Housework by Better Equipment*, published in 1929.

▲ This wooden bread plate was hand-carved in the late 1930s. It depicts the Oakland Bay Bridge in San Francisco, USA, which was completed in 1936.

£25–30

◀ Made in France, this is a 19th-century cheeseboard decorated with small brass star-shaped studs, which would have been found in a cheese shop on the display counter. It has a deep narrow trench around the edge where originally there was a domed glass cover.

£45–60

▲ A wonderful find, this breadboard looks brand new and still has its price tag attached on the back, although it was made in the 1930s.

£10–15

▶ The blade of the Victorian knife (top) is etched with a typically fancy design. In the centre is a later 19th century knife with a fine serrated edge. The bottom knife has a blade with larger serrations and a pointed tip. It was made from the 1940s to the 1950s.

£5–20

▶ This is a Dutch serving board for passing around sausages at the table. It has been carefully carved with a heart, suggesting it was originally made as a love token. Note the the heart shape is repeated in the handle and the fine serrated edge. It is unusual to find such a traditional Dutch board outside Holland.

£20–30

OTHER TOOLS

The first fruit corers were made from the shank-bones of sheep and date back to the early Middle Ages. Primitive and plain in design, they changed little until the 17th century. The basic shape comprised a handle and a scoop, carved to a point. As tooth decay was so prevalent, these utensils were often used to scoop soft flesh from the fruit by people who had lost their teeth !

By the 18th and 19th centuries, corers were made of boxwood, sycamore, ivory, lignum vitae and even silver. The design altered, comprising a single piece with an elongated handle, and the scoop had a rounded end.

By the late 19th century, steel was used to make the blade, and handles were made of wood, while by the 1920s they were mass-produced from various materials.

The first mechanical apple parer (for peeling apples) is thought to have been invented by an American, Moses Coates, in 1803, but the first patent for a machine for peeling and coring apples mechanically was taken out in 1873 by 'Messrs Landers, Frary & Clark' of Boston, USA. Homemade parers became an American speciality in the early 19th century, and were produced in large numbers.

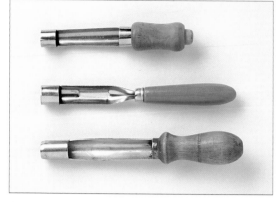

▲ This group of apple corers dates from the 1920s to 1950s and are of varying quality. The corer with the boxwood handle (top) was made in the late 1920s. It is known as the 'two-in-one' reversible corer, as the stubby handle fits the ends of the corer – one end for large apples, the other for small ones.

By contrast, the corer in the centre is poorly constructed. Lightweight and flimsy, it has a stainless steel corer and was made in the late 1950s.

The handle of the third corer was originally painted red. An unsuccessful attempt at stripping it has left an unpleasant stain and reduced its appeal.

Under £7 each

◄ Unusual gadgets are fun to collect, such as this cast-iron raisin seeder from North America. Made by the firm Enterprise Mfg. Co., based in Philadelphia, USA, it would have been used in a domestic kitchen to seed raisins – a laborious and tiring task when done by hand. This one has survived in good condition; if it had suffered too much rust damage, the value would be lowered. As often happened, Britain imported the American version of an item for several years and then produced their own copy. The first British raisin seeder was patented in 1898 and was called a raisin stoner.

£45–65

▼ The French company Mouli advertised the larger chopping machine (below, left) as 'the most amazing machine for chopping parsley, mint, herbs, eggs, orange and lemon peel', in the 1950s. Early examples, from the 1930s, had wooden handles, but, by the 1950s, handles were made from plastic.

At one time this 1930s hand mincer (right), also called a parsley chopper would have had a coloured handle, but at some stage it has been stripped, possibly by a dealer, to give it a 'cottage pine' look.

Left: £6–9 **Right: £5–8**

▲ Made in Sweden, this is a clamp-style apple corer and parer from the late 1930s. Remarkably, this one has never been used and was found wrapped in the paper in which it was bought. Produced by a number of makers throughout Europe and North America, these peelers are very collectable today. Beware of identical modern versions.

£20–25

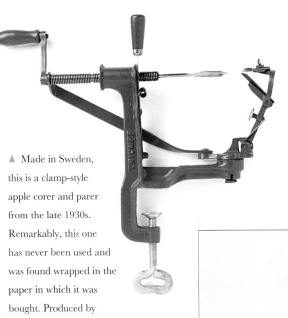

◄ The tinned steel food mincer (left) is known as a 'Moulinette'. Available in the early 1930s, it was made with three cutting discs and different-coloured handles (red, dark green, cream and blue). A versatile tool, it was advertised as suitable for 'mincing and chopping fish, suet, vegetables and fruit, preparing paste for sandwiches, stuffing, small pieces of raw and cooked meat'. The mincer also had an ingenious pressure regulator, which prevented too much pressure being put on the blades, which could break them.

The Mouli grater (right) was made in this shape from the late 1950s to the early 1960s. The design had been available since the 1930s with a wooden handle and it is still produced today, but made of plastic, apart from the drum section.

It is an ingenious device and easy to use. Cheese, nutmeg, bread, chocolate and nuts can all be grated; it is ideal for grating small amounts, but time-consuming for larger quantities.

Left: £14–18 **Right: £6–8**

CUTLERY

Before the 20th century, kitchen cutlery, particularly knives and forks, would have been made of iron by a local blacksmith, who would repair it when necessary. In North America tin was used as well, although the Pennsylvania Dutch were making wrought-iron pancake turners, spatulas and meat forks from the early 18th century onwards.

In the same period in Britain polished horn spoons with long handles were popular, used mainly for stirring eggs and cream mixtures and also for spooning syrups. More expensive than metal or wooden cutlery, they would be used only for special baking, such as making Easter or Christmas cakes, and not in everyday cooking.

By the late 19th century, aluminium was used, mainly in North America, although Germany was also a prolific manufacturer of aluminium utensils between 1900 and the 1930s. This period saw an explosion in the variety of cutlery and items were mass-produced. Spoons were made in numerous shapes, such as basting spoons, tasting spoons and snipe ladles; while slices, tin-openers, and whisks also became widely available.

The 20th century saw further variations, such as slotted and perforated spoons, made of tin, wood, metal or aluminium.

Kitchen cutlery has always been multi-purpose, making it one of the most versatile as well as practical fields to collect.

▼ A Victorian tinned-steel fish slice.

LADLES & TASTING SPOONS

Ladles were traditionally made from a wide range of materials, including pewter, brass, and, from the 19th century onwards, steel and enamel. From this period wooden handles were added too. As well as round or oval-shaped ladles, look out for side-snipe ladles, which have a lip and were best for pouring.

Tasting spoons and ladles along with other utensils have always been hung up close at hand to the cooking area when not in use. By the 1850s, special racks were made and in the late 19th century these incorporated a trough at the bottom to catch any drips. Initially, they were made in wrought iron, then enamelled iron and later from stamped sheet aluminium (until the 1930s). Aluminium racks often featured embossed designs; hunting and shooting scenes were popular in Germany, while windmills were found in Holland and decorative designs such as feathers and sprays in France.

The most colourful and collectable enamel racks were made in Belgium, Germany and Holland in the early 20th century.

▲ At the top is a 1900s American stamped-tin tasting spoon, with a suitably deep and curved bow. Below is a Victorian tinned-steel basting spoon. The perforated spoon (second from bottom) was made in Belgium from the 1930s to 1940s, while the American slotted spoon (bottom) is a good example of an American cake mixer spoon.

£8–14 each

◀ This French aluminium utensil rack has echoes of Art Nouveau in its design embossed into a sheet of aluminium. Originally, it would have had a set of three utensils.

£24–30

◄ Made in France, this red enamel utensil rack still has its original set of three matching utensils: a skimmer. a soup ladle and a side-snipe ladle. The rack has been beautifully designed and is in excellent condition, which is reflected in its price.

£75–100

▼ Dating from the mid-19th century to the 1960s, this selection shows a good range. Spoons with holes can be used to add extra air to batter; long flat spoons are ideal for scraping bowls, while slotted ones can be used to serve and drain.

£2–7 each

▼ This group of spoons includes a Dutch grey mottled enamel ladle from the 1930s (bottom left). Above it is a French mixing spoon from the 1920s. At the top left is an American tasting spoon from the 1920s and to its right is a Dutch ladle, also from the 1920s. The ladle on the far right was made in North America from the 1930s to the 1940s.

£15–20 each

WOODEN SPOONS

Wooden spoons and rolling pins were originally carved by hand at home. Made from strong, inflexible hard woods, such as beech, sycamore, ash and olive, they were used for a variety of jobs, such as mixing and stirring. Mass production began in the 19th century, in both Europe and North America, and until the 1920s, spoons were available in only one shape, with the handle and bowl generally carved separately. From 1920 onwards, different designs were introduced, based on the shapes of steel and iron spoons, and they were mass-produced from one piece of wood. The shape and size of a wooden spoon is important, as it is closely linked to its purpose. Early spoons often had a ball-end on the handle, used to settle fruit and vegetables in preserving jars and to help shape a cottage loaf in bread-making. In Britain and North America wooden spoons with thick scooped-out bowls are used to stir and beat. In France, flat rectangular spatulas are commonly used, as they fit the flat-bottomed mixing bowls used in a French kitchen.

DRAINING & STRAINING CUTLERY

Over the centuries cutlery for draining food, for skimming fat off meat stews and soups or for lifting food from boiling liquids has been called by a variety of names. In the 17th century a skimming implement, a ladle with crudely punched holes in the base and used to remove the scum from soups, was appropriately known as a scummer; while, in the 18th century, the name was changed to skimmer. Tin skimmers were made in the late 19th century until the 1900s. Enamel was popular in this century, as was aluminium.

▲ Trowel-shaped slices are specifically for fish and are distinguished from egg slices by their rounder blades. This group of fish slices includes a British white enamel fish slice made from the 1920s to the 1930s (top) and a 1900s fish slice (second from top). Note that earlier versions have a wider blade and a more pronounced curve on the top of the blade. The bottom slice (bottom) has the Diamond Brand trademark and was made from 1910. Note how similar in shape it is to the 1900s one above. On the right is an Edwardian fish slice with a long blue handle. Its perforations have been designed into a fish shape and the blade's flat front is ideal for sliding under a fish.

£7–25 each

◄ There is a lovely perforated pattern in the small round bowl of this enamel strainer ladle (far left). Also called a pea strainer, this one was made in North America in the 1900s. Although it is slightly chipped, it is so desirable the chips do not lower its value. To its right is a rare American enamel skimmer made in the 1870s. Second from the right is a 1930s Dutch skimmer. It is still in perfect condition and has an attractive green painted handle. On the far right is another American skimmer-strainer, made in the 1900s. It has an unusual shallow bowl with perforations. The pattern of this enamel ware is known as 'chicken wire'.

£10–35 each

◄ Made in Spain in the 1950s, this is an olive strainer for lifting olives out of a jar. The hook hangs from the side of an olive jar.

£8–12

▼ The unusual shape of the tinned steel bowl adds greatly to the appeal of this rare skimmer made in Britain in the 1860s.

£30–40

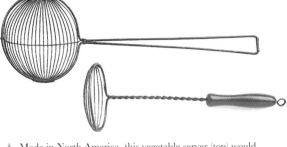

▲ Made in North America, this vegetable server (top) would greatly appeal to wirework collectors. Beautifully made from twisted wire, it is both practical and attractive. Below is an American pea server from the same period, which is even more desirable. Both are in excellent condition.

Top: £14–18 **Bottom: £16–20**

► This selection of slices, from left to right, includes an unusually small, 2in (5cm) wide, Skyline egg slice from the 1930s to the 1940s. To its right is an aluminium egg slice from the 1950s. A large heavy duty 1940s fish slice (third from left) has a pretty perforated blade and next to it is a Victorian slice which has been retinned. Second from the right is a 1930s egg slice with a stripped white wooden handle. The slice on the far right is an aluminium cake turner with a perforated blade.

£5–25 each

ENAMEL KITCHENWARE

Enamelling has been an art form since the Ancient Chinese first practised it in the Tang Dynasty (AD 618-906). However, the mid-19th century saw the first commercial use of enamelling on metals with the mass production of enamelled cookware, known as enamelware in Britain and graniteware in North America. Various metals have been successfully enamelled, in particular iron and steel, and hard-wearing and attractive utensils were produced in a variety of colours and patterns. Appropriate names were adopted for the different patterns, such as splatter, mottle, feathered, shaded and chickenwire. Whereas countries such as Britain, Yugoslavia and Poland preferred plain and simple designs, France, Germany and Holland produced more imaginative and colourful pieces.

Pre-1960s enamelware is widely collected. Condition is important, but chips are acceptable, so long as they do not come into contact with food.

EGG BEATERS & WHISKS

Although wire balloon whisks have been a perennial favourite with cooks since the end of the 18th century, it was the invention of the rotary egg beater in the early 20th century, one of the first new kitchen gadgets to enter the kitchen for nearly 250 years, that had the most impact on the development of kitchenware utensils.

The rotary egg beater, so called because it works by turning a handle, was capable of whisking food much faster and with less effort than hand whisks. The rotary mechanism was soon applied to a range of other cooking utensils, such as cake mixers, food blenders and bread makers.

▲ This selection of whisks dates from the 1900s to the 1920s and includes three 'Archimedean' screw-type whisks. These work by pressing the knob up and down, which curls or twists the whisk part. The one with the green handle was made in the 1920s, while the version with the turned wooden handle dates from the 1900s. This is more valuable as it has an attractive wire arrangement. The third 'Archimedean' whisk on the right dates from the 1920s. Nutbrown made the spiral whisk (second from right) from the 1930s to the 1950s.

£12–25 each

WHISK OR BEATER?

In Britain, hand and rotary whisks have been called a variety of names, such as egg whisks, batter beaters and egg beaters.

In North America, it is much simpler; rotary whisks (with handles) are called egg beaters, while those without handles are called whisks. Both countries produced a wide variety of each.

▶ Early whisks were generally made out of twisted wire. These three are American and date from the 1880s to the early 1900s.

£10–18 each

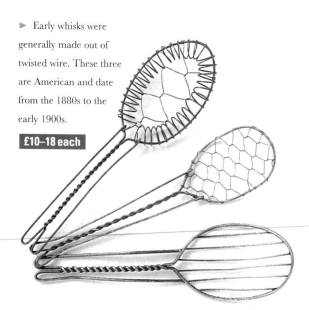

North America was a prolific producer of rotary egg beaters and exported many to Europe in the 19th century. From the early 20th century onwards, Europe made their own, often copying American designs.

A tip when choosing a rotary whisk is always to turn the handle several times to check the blades or loops have not become twisted or out of line. Do this by holding the beater upright; if you hold it upside down, the air will prevent it from turning smoothly.

Other types of beaters and whisks that are now collectable include a special spoon available in the late 1920s that was capable of separating the white from the yolk of an egg and could also be used for beating eggs, stirring sauces, draining and serving.

In spite of the choice of whisks available, many kitchens simply used an ordinary household fork for beating.

▲ These two whisks were made in the 1930s. The one on the left, made by an unknown manufacturer, was also available with blue or green handles and was ideal for heavy beating. On the right is a Skyline rotary whisk with four double blades. The mechanism still works smoothly.

Left: £12–15 **Right: £10–15**

▶ These light wire whisks include two small handy whisks (left) made by numerous manufacturers from the 1930s to the 1950s. In the centre is a tinned-wire balloon whisk made in the 1930s, advertising Bournville cocoa. The band of wire around the end adjusts the width of the whisk to fit the size of the bowl or cup that is used. Look out for an earlier promotional whisk by Bournville, brought out in 1910, which has more wire loops and a plain wood handle. Second from the right is a 1930s wire whisk offered as a wire egg bat or beater. This one was a favourite and was produced in large numbers, some carrying advertisements, such as 'Bird's Spongie Mix'. One the far right is a 1900s balloon whisk, similar to today's, but stronger.

£5–15 each

OTHER KITCHEN GADGETS

The variety of kitchen utensils made over the past 100 years is enormous, reflecting the number of jobs carried out in the kitchen. The design of many items, such as nutcrackers or pepper-mills, have not changed greatly over the years, an indication of their usefulness and durability. However, there are also pieces that did not stand the test of time or were superseded, such as early tin openers, yet they are all worth collecting.

Among the wide range of gadgets to look out for are ice cream wafer holders and cheese testers. Many knives are collectable, including specially designed knives for opening oysters or for segmenting grapefruit.

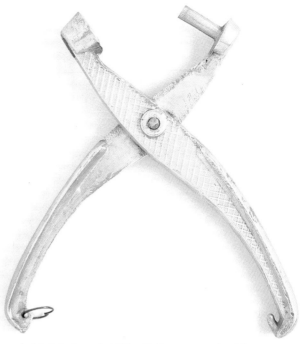

▲ Made in the early 1930s, this German cast-aluminium gadget is used for stoning cherries or olives. The fruit is placed in the indentation and then the spike pushed down on to it which presses out the stone. Lightweight stainless steel versions are made today and are not collectable. Earlier ones are better made – note the brass rivet in the centre to add strength to the joint. Look out for a cast-iron cherry pipper brought out in North America in 1860.

£6–8

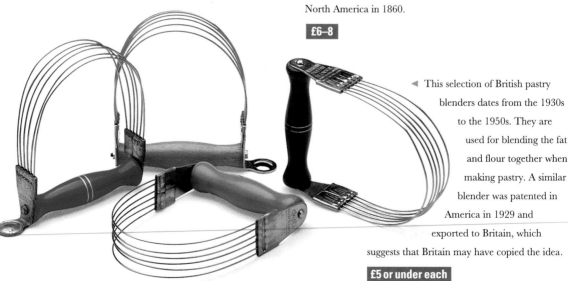

◄ This selection of British pastry blenders dates from the 1930s to the 1950s. They are used for blending the fat and flour together when making pastry. A similar blender was patented in America in 1929 and exported to Britain, which suggests that Britain may have copied the idea.

£5 or under each

▼ Made in the 1930s, this attractive wooden pepper-mill in the form of a lighthouse comes from France. The checks are formed from sections of wood and the red parts have been painted with an enamel paint. It works using a typical pepper-mill mechanism: turning the top part activates the blades at the bottom which cut up the peppercorns. This one is a rare piece; it is not marked with a maker's name and was possibly a tourist souvenir.

£30–40

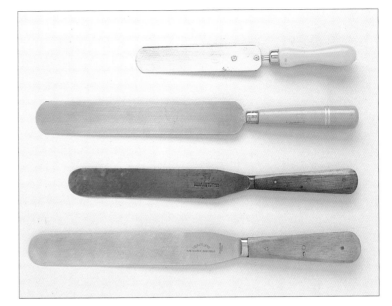

▲ This selection of palette knives and spreaders (known as spatulas in North America) dates from the 19th century to the 1950s. They are useful for many baking jobs as the blades are flexible enough to clean round a mixing bowl, and spread icing on top of cakes or fillings into large sponge cakes.

Early knives such as the Victorian one (second from bottom) are highly prized, reflected in their value.

Victorian knife: £8–12
Other knives: £6 or under

▼ Ballers are used for making attractive spherical shapes of vegetables (for garnishing soups) or butter. Vegetable ballers appeared in the 19th century, with melon and butter ballers following in the 20th century. At the top is an English tin vegetable baller, made in the 1900s. It is a particularly appealing example as it comprises two different sized ballers. The baller with the yellow wooden handle was made by Tala from the 1930s to the 1940s.

£5–7 each

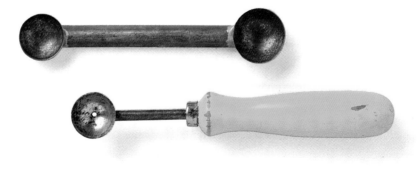

◄ This nickel-plated pair of nutcrackers (left) dates from the 1920s. Note that at the top of the inside of the handles there should be a ridged jaw to grip and hold the nut, in position.

This simple but effective design continues to be produced, though they are rarely nickel-plated today.

£5–8

► Produced from the 1950s to the 1960s, this pair of nutcrackers is by Nutbrown. They differ greatly from the late 19th-century pair (above). The top part is hinged with rivets and is able to crack all sizes of nut. Remarkably, not many were produced.

£6–8

OPENERS

The idea of keeping food for a long time in a 'vacuum' goes back to the 18th century. But it was not until 1810 that a patent was taken out in London for the canning process. North America maintains that the first successful tin (called a can in North America) was made there, invented by Thomas Kensitt in 1813, while Britain argues that it was made in a cannery owned by Donkin & Hall of Bermondsey, London, in 1812.

Soon a massive industry existed, devoted to producing tinned food, and, with it, came the problem of opening tins. Early methods were very basic – tins came with instructions which advised the user to cut round the top near the outer edge with a hammer and chisel! The introduction of the first tin-opener by the 1870s was a major advance. One of the best-known in this period was launched in 1875 by J.A. Wilson of Chicago, USA, who sold it with their newly introduced tinned corned beef, known as bully beef.

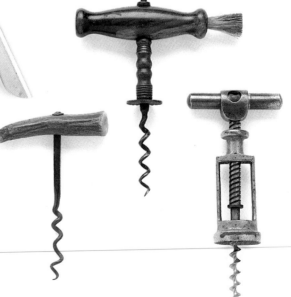

► Corkscrews are a highly popular collecting field today. As many designs were made and in large numbers, condition is important. Always check the screw part is correct; on the one on the left it has become bent and distorted, which lowers the value. Victorian butlers' corkscrews (centre) often incorporate a pure bristle brush (for brushing dirt off the tops of bottles). This is a particularly fine example and has an attractive wooden handle. Made in the 1920s, the corkscrew on the right is known as 'The Monopol' and is a self-pulling corkscrew.

£10–45

▶ This selection of tin-openers includes (top) a steel cutter. Made in the 1890s, it carries the brand name Fentons, and adjusts to any size tin. Below is a scissor-pattern opener, called the 'P.C.', after the first letters of the surnames of A.H.F. Pearl and R.H. Carter of London who patented the design in 1922.

Also from the 1920s is the tin-opener in the centre of the picture, which incorporates a bottle-opener. The sharp tip on the opener is used to pierce the tin so the contents can be poured out. An unusual item, the opener at the bottom is used for piercing tins and opening bottles. It is stamped *CERVEZA SCHLAU*, Spanish for 'clever beer', which is unusual as it is also stamped 'Made in USA'. It is a gem for bottle-opener collectors, and this is reflected in its value.

£8–15 each

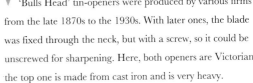

▼ Sadly, the paint on the wooden handle of the smallest opener (top) has been stripped off. Originally, it would have been available in green or red. Incorporating both a bottle- and a tin-opener, it was made in the 1940s. Its design is clumsy as the handle is too small and chunky to hold properly.

In the centre is a Skyline tin- and bottle- opener. Although not of very high value, this item is well-made. Similar designs are produced today. Even sardine tin-openers are collectable! This one (bottom) was made in the 1920s.

£5 or under each

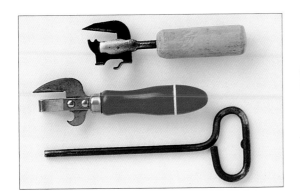

▼ 'Bulls Head' tin-openers were produced by various firms from the late 1870s to the 1930s. With later ones, the blade was fixed through the neck, but with a screw, so it could be unscrewed for sharpening. Here, both openers are Victorian; the top one is made from cast iron and is very heavy.

£20–25 each

▼ Spurtles are traditional Scottish kitchen utensils, used for stirring porridge to make a smooth texture and to prevent it from sticking to the pan. A similar utensil, called a porridge stirrer, was used in the north of England to a lesser extent, , but these were simple plain-waisted sticks.

This selection of spurtles dates from the early 19th century to the present day. Early spurtles were plain and simple, waisted at the top end to form a grip with plain rounded ends. Later, the knobs developed into thistle tops. Second from the top is a modern spurtle. Although not yet collectable, it has been included to show how elaborate they have become.

£10–25 each

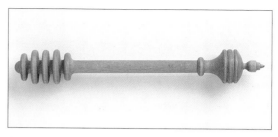

▲ This elegant late 19th-century honey stick is put into the honey pot and, when turned and lifted out, the honey holds between the ridges and can be dripped on to bread or toast.

£12–15

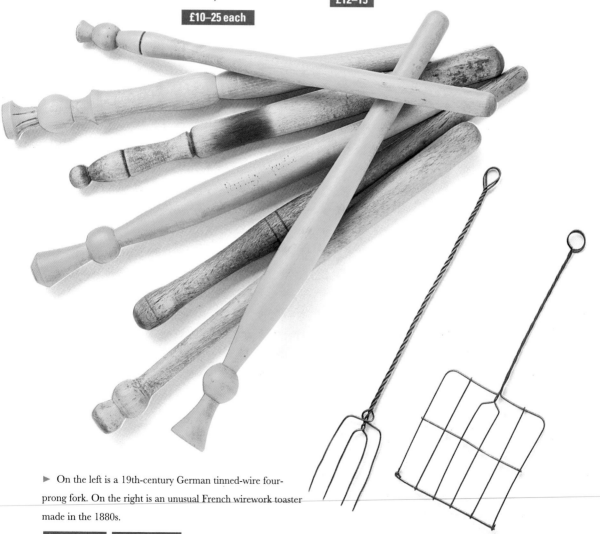

► On the left is a 19th-century German tinned-wire four-prong fork. On the right is an unusual French wirework toaster made in the 1880s.

Left: £15–18   **Right: £18–25**

FORKS

It is worth remembering that forks were not used for eating until the 18th century, although large forks have long played an important role in the kitchen. Early forks were used for toasting and roasting food in front of an open fire. Made from iron, brass, and, by the 19th century, steel, they typically had fairly longish handles often with some decoration.

Toasting forks were popular by the 18th century; American toasters of the late 18th century could be revolved so both sides of the bread could be toasted. European toasting forks differed and were held by long handles. By the 20th century two types of fork had developed: sharp, pointed forks for meat, and toasting forks which had blunt ends.

▶ On the left is top-of-the-range French cooks' fork, used in all types of cooking. Made from the 1920s to the 1930, it was also available with a black wooden handle without a guard. The large fork next to it is British Army issue from the 1940s, identified by the arrow on the back of the handle. All H.M. forces issue items had an arrow on them to prevent them from being sold on to civilians. This example is in good condition and would be of considerable interest to collectors of War Issue and utility items. On the right are two Skyline two-pronged meat forks. The one with the homemade hook dates from the 1930s, the other from the 1940s.

£5–15 each

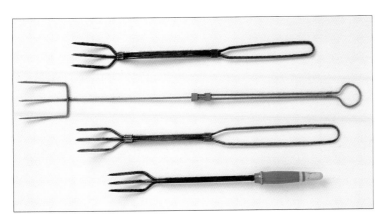

◀ The green-handled Skyline fork (bottom) was offered as a meat fork and was made from the 1930s to the early 1940s. Above is a three-pronged kitchen fork, made from the 1900s to the 1930s, while the large fork is a three-pronged extending toasting fork (shown extended). At the top is a strong tinned-wire flesh fork, made from the 1900s to the 1930s.

£5–9 each

123

KITCHEN EQUIPMENT

As the traditional centre of activity in a household for centuries the kitchen was a place of hard work and uncomfortable conditions. It was not until the 19th century that any special aids or equipment were developed to assist with the many tasks that accompany cooking and preparing food, such as lighting fires, cleaning stoves and washing up.

Until the 19th century, washing up in most homes was carried out simply with hot water and the occasional scouring with sand – soap had been available since the 16th century, but could be afforded only by the wealthy. In the 18th and early 19th centuries the kitchen sink was usually made of stone or hard wood with a pipe to discharge the dirty water outside the house. As there were no drains, the waste often soaked away into the

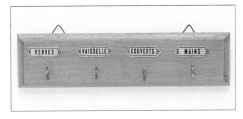

▲ A French cloth holder, made in the 1920s.

ground; sewage systems were not developed until the mid-19th century.

Conditions gradually improved – soap became plentiful following the repeal of duty on it in 1853; soda, a derivative of soap, was also introduced and became widely used for washing laundry. Fire-lighting became easier too, with the invention of sulphur matches in the early 19th century.

In the 20th century, soda was replaced by washing powder and soap by washing-up liquid, while electricity led to a wide range of labour-saving equipment such as washing machines.

SCULLERY ITEMS

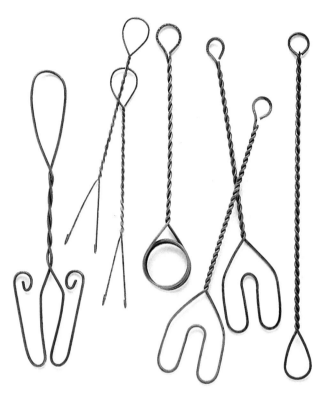

Washing up has always been considered a menial and unpopular task, usually carried out by the most junior servant in the house. By the 18th and 19th centuries, in wealthy homes washing up took place in the scullery in a large stone sink, while poorer homes used a large metal bowl.

Few implements were available until the late 19th century, but the 20th century saw many improvements.

◄ Wirework implements such as these, made in England and North America from the 1800s to 1940s, are often wrongly identified as whisks. In fact, they are dishcloth holders (known as dishtowel holders in North America), which, in spite of their unglamorous use, were often elaborately designed. Originally, the holders would have held coloured strips of cotton rags.

Under £5 each

▼ The ivory-coloured bowl (left) would have been used both as a small laundry bowl and for doing the washing up. Various colours were available; ivory with blue relief, ivory with scarlet relief, silvery green with black relief and white with blue relief. On the right is a shallow Dutch 'wash-up' bowl. They were not exported abroad, so are rare today. Remarkably, both bowls are in good condition; they often suffer wear and tear.

Left: £10–14   **Right: £14–£20**

WASHING-UP BOWLS

Made of enamelled iron and steel, washing-up bowls came in various sizes and shapes. Produced in North America from the 1870s onwards and in Britain from the 1890s onwards, they were placed inside a stone sink as a way of using less hot water and so conserving fuel. Shallow oval washing-up bowls with handles at the sides are common in continental Europe, while Britain and North America use round ones. Condition can vary; feel inside the bowl, as years of using soda can take the sheen off.

▲ Made in France, this dark blue enamel soap dish was also available in white. Always make sure the dish still has its drainer, as it is less valuable without it.

£8–12

▼ This French red box with gilt lettering is used to store soda crystals for washing. Made for the domestic market ('soda' means the same in French), it was part of a wide range of household utensils in this colour and design, such as the cutlery hanging rack shown on p.113. Few soda boxes exist, as many have been destroyed by the soda which corrodes the metal.

On the left is a French *allumette* (match) container made from the 1900s to the 1920s; similar versions were available in Britain and North America. This box would have been kept near the cooking area. Early versions often incorporated a striking strip on the top or inside the lid. The orange and white colouring is rare, as is aqua and white, 'old' red and white or blue and white, all in the much sought after 'feather' pattern.

Left: £28–36
Right: £35–45

▼ The cylindrical cutlery drainer (left) is rare and was made from the 1920s to the 1930s. In the centre is a Jury Brand sink tidy from the 1930s to the 1950s. The ivory-coloured Judge Brand sink tidy (right) dates from the late 1920s.

Left: £18–24 **Centre: £10–14** **Right: £12–14**

SINK TIDIES

Sink tidies, also called sink baskets, were first available in the 1900s. They are triangular in shape so they can lodge neatly in the corner of a traditional glazed earthenware sink, and are used to scrape waste into (from plates and teapots for example) before washing up the dishes. At one time all the waste would be burnt on the kitchen fire – an inexpensive form of fuel.

Sink tidies are used in all European countries and made from enamelled iron or steel, although aluminium ones were also produced.

▶ The shopping basket has been a regular feature in all kitchens for centuries. Made of willow, this one is late Edwardian and is still in good condition. A popular material for baskets, willow grows in marshy areas. Planted in the spring and harvested in the summer, willow gave seasonal employment to whole families who cut, stripped and prepared it. This pattern of growing and weaving remained the same from the 15th century to the eve of World War I, resulting in a wide range of baskets for all types of household use, from picnic hampers to laundry baskets.

Later baskets (from the 1920s onwards) are less collectable, so look out for ones with a patina acquired from use over many years or other signs of wear and tear. Many baskets will have undergone some sort of home repair, which will lower the value, but often adds appeal.

£20–30 each

STORING CUTLERY

Traditionally, knives were counted as among the most valuable items of a household, along with candles and matches. The earliest knife boxes resembled salt boxes, but were much deeper inside. The box would have been hung by the fire to keep the blades dry.

From the early 19th century, knife boxes were wider and flatter, with two hinged lids on either side of a carrying handles and stored knives, forks and spoons. They were made from a variety of woods, including mahogany and oak, and were often decorated.

▼ Made in France, this knife basket (also called a cutlery basket) from the 1920s was used to carry cutlery from the kitchen to the dining-room to lay the table and for storing knives and forks when not in use. The wicker is worked up from the hardwood base to form a basket with a centre division – one side for knives, the other for forks.

The attractive 'blue' colour was achieved by painting the basket with enamel paint. Overall, the basket is in very good condition (even complete with its original lining) and is collectable. Note that in North America all types of cutlery containers are called cutlery trays.

£15–20

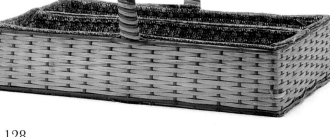

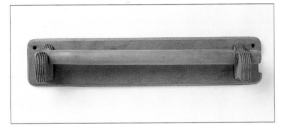

▲ This delicate 19th-century French wirework wall rack was used to hang either dishcloths or utensils; it is too flimsy for coats or other clothes. Often elaborately made, such as this one, they are now highly sought after by wirework collectors, and this is reflected in their value. They were available in various sizes; some had as many as 10 hooks, while others had just one single hook.

£25–30

▲ Although similar in design to modern versions, this wooden towel roller dates from the late 19th century. The towel would have been made of huckaback (a type of rough linen fabric) and could be bought ready to use or as a strip of fabric and sewn up at home. The bracket would have been put up in the scullery or kitchen near to the sink area or behind the kitchen door.

£16–£24

► Before the successful introduction of electric kettles in 1921, most homes used stove kettles to boil water – the term kettle originally referred to a type of large general-purpose cooking pan. It later became known as a tea kettle, as it was gradually used only for boiling water for tea. This kettle, made of enamelled iron, dates from the 1930s. Although made in Sweden, it was widely exported abroad. This one has a 4 pint (2.24 litre) capacity; they were also available in sizes up to a 20 pint (12 litre) capacity for use in schools and other institutions.

£15–20

► Written by an English colonist, Mrs. St. John Hodson, who lived in Barbados in the 1940s, *War Time Recipes for use in the West Indies* is a fascinating selection of recipes and an interesting reflection of social attitudes at the time – note how a West Indian is pictured doing the cooking.

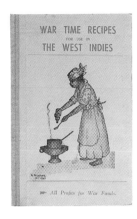

£20–25

MRS. BEETON (1836–1865)

Mrs. Beeton was born Isabella Mayson in 1836. In 1856 she married Samuel Orchard Beeton, a publisher. She became a household name after the publication of her *Household Management*. It was first published in several parts (1859–60) in a women's magazine founded by her husband, which covered cookery and other branches of domestic science.

COOKERY BOOKS

Cookery books offer a fascinating insight into the development of cooking and complement any collection of kitchenware. It was the Victorians who instigated the great rise in the number of cook books and books on household management, and all but the rarest books are reasonably priced. In addition to famous writers such as Mrs. Beeton, collectable names include Eliza Acton (1799–1859) who published *Modern Cookery for Private Families* in 1845. First editions of both authors are the most expensive, but numerous reprints are available for much less.

From the 20th century, works by Elizabeth David and Jane Grigson are the most collectable. For many,

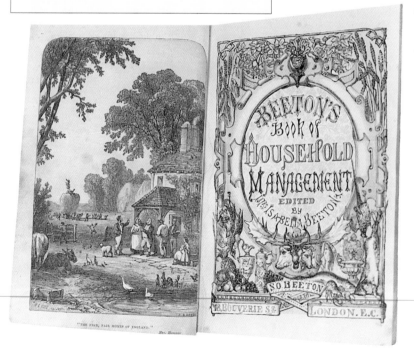

◄ Leather-bound first editions of Mrs. Beeton's *Book of Household Management*, published in 1861, are highly sought after today by collectors. A huge success since it was first published, it was originally aimed at young middle-class Victorian wives who did not employ many servants. Her recipes always included the cost, cooking time and number of servings.

£300–£400

these two authors radically changed the whole nature of cooking, and their books form a strong starting point for a collector. Elizabeth David's cookery books often feature an attractive dust jacket 'decorated', as he called it, by John Minton, and can still be found priced under £100. Jane Grigson's works are more recent but already classics in their own right. As with collecting all types of books, there is a premium for a fine-jacketed copy as opposed to a worn one and many collectors prefer the addition of contemporary notes.

At the bottom end of the range, recent cookery books written by less well-known cooks are fun to collect and can often be found for only a few pounds.

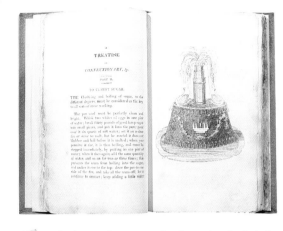

▲ Among the most sought after cookery books is the *Treatise on Confectionery in all its Branches* by Joseph Bell. It was privately published in 1817 and has a section on making different ice creams.

£200–400

◀ This book, published in the 1960s, has been signed by Lady Clementine Spencer Churchill, wife of the former British Prime Minister, Sir Winston Churchill, which boosts its value.

Under £5

◀ *Mediterranean and French Country Food,* one of many cookery books written by Elizabeth David, was first published in 1951. The attractive cover was designed by the illustrator John Minton.

£10–£15

▶ *Cook Now, Dine Later* by Catherine Althaus and Peter ffrench-Hodges featured many imaginative recipes and was a hugely popular cookery book in the late 1960s and early 1970s. The design of the cover is typical of this period and adds greatly to the book's appeal.

Under £5

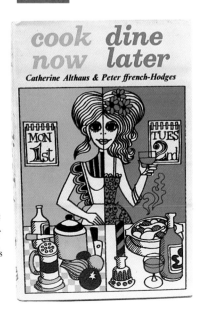

MAKERS

ALUMINIUM GOODS MANUFACTURING CO.
Established in 1909 and still active today. Possibly one of the earliest North American kitchenware makers still to exist.

ASH BROS. & HEATON LTD.
Makers of copper kitchen moulds active in the 19th century.

BALDWIN
19th-century manufacturers of coffee grinders, based in Southport in Lancashire.

BETTERWEAR
Founded in 1929, they were early pioneers of doorstep selling. They produced all types of household items and gadgets. Still active as Betterwear UK Ltd. and based in Birmingham.

BIRD'S
Major manufacturers of convenience foods. Established in 1837 by Alfred Bird, the company are best known for their wide range of jellies and custards.

JOSEPH BOURNE & SON
Established in 1812 and still active today, they are among Britain's major stoneware producers. They are best known for their Denbyware range of household pottery.

CENTRAL STATES MANUFACTURING CO.
Based in St. Louis, USA and makers of aluminium gadgets.

CROWN MERTON
Producers of high-quality aluminium hollow ware from the 1920s to the 1950s.

DALEWARE
Trade name for brand of aluminium hollow ware made between 1910 and the 1930s.

DOULTON & CO.
Founded in 1835 in Lambeth, south London, producing stoneglaze sewage pipes, sanitary- and kitchenware. The pottery gradually expanded to include terracotta sculpture from the turn of the century onwards. In 1902, the company were renamed Royal Doulton.

ENTERPRISE MANUFACTURING CO.
Based in Philadelphia in the late 19th century, they produced a range of gadgets, including meat choppers, sausage stuffers, lard pressers and raisin seeders.

GUARDIAN FRIGERATION CO.
Makers of domestic refrigerators since 1919.

H.J. GREEN & CO. LTD.
Grocers suppliers, based in Brighton in Sussex from 1910-1960. They sold a range of cooking equipment embossed with their company name.

T. & GREEN & CO.
Makers of kitchenware pottery since the mid-1860s, their best-known range is the Cornishware series of blue-and-white-striped pottery. First produced in the 1930s, Cornishware was originally sold exclusively through F.W. Woolworth in Britain.

GUARDIAN FRIGERATOR COMPANY
North American manufacturers of domestic refrigerators since c.1919, later becoming the Frigidaire Corporation.

JOBLINGS
One of the largest mineral merchants and suppliers of glass-making chemicals in the north of England. From 1921 onwards, they owned the sole rights to manufacture Pyrex products thoughout the British Empire, apart from Canada.

KENRICK
Archibald Kenrick established an iron foundry in 1815, specializing in making a wide range of household products. The firm are most famous for their coffee grinders, first patented in 1815 and widely copied by other makers throughout the 19th century. The firm later became known as Kenrick & Sons.

LEE & WILKES
Major producers of kitchen moulds, they were established as Birch & Villers in 1780, becoming Villers & Wilkes in 1818. In 1907 the firm joined with Charles Lee and became Lee & Wilkes.

LOVATT'S
Established in 1895 in Nottingham, Lovatt's were major British manufacturers of earthenware pottery.

MADE RITE
Based in London and Blackpool, Made Rite produced a wide range of inexpensive kitchen gadgets in the 1950s, describing themselves as 'domestic equipment specialists', producing 'kitchen aids for the modern housewife'.

MEREDITH & DREW LTD.
Based in Scotland, this firm were leading biscuit makers from the late 19th-mid-20th century. In the 1940s they joined McVitie's, a division of United Biscuits. They also produced biscuit jars.

PRIDE-O-HOME
Pride-O-Home was the promotional slogan for Homepride, one of Britain's leading brands of flour. Established in the 1920s, Homepride, owned by Fosters, were originally called Tommy Homepride Mills and they were based in Cambridge, Coventry and Birkenhead. Between 1922 and 1923, Homepride produced a range of promotional kitchenware all marked with the 'Pride-O-Home' slogan. Fosters were taken over by Spillers in 1949, becoming Dalgety-Spillers Food Ltd. in the 1960s.

NUTBROWN
Established in Blackpool in 1927 and dissolved in 1988, Nutbrown were major British kitchenware manufacturers.

PLATERS & STAMPERS
Based in Burnley in Lancashire from the 1930s to the 1950s, Platers & Stampers are best known for their Skyline range of utensils and gadgets, although they also made bathroom fittings.

ROBERTSON'S
One of Britain's most famous manufacturers of preserves and jams. The company was set up by James Robertson, a grocer, in the 1860s. Producing a wide range of jams, preserves and mincemeat, they became virtually synonymous with their Golly trademark, introduced in 1910.

SALTER
Leading makers of weighing scales since 1760.

SMITH'S POTATO CRISPS LTD.
Established in 1920 by Frank Smith, Smith's Potato Crisps has become among Britain's most successful potato crisps manufacturers.

TALA
Tala is the trade name of Taylor, Law & Co. Ltd. established in the late 1890s. Originally based in Birmingham and later at Stourbridge, Tala were major manufacturers of tin gadgets and utensils. Producing a wide range of good-quality products they were fierce rivals to Nutbrown (see above). The Tala brand name is today used by George East Housewares.

GLOSSARY

ALUMINIUM
A type of metal invented in Denmark by H.C. Oerstedt in 1825. It was first used to make domestic hollow ware from the late 19th century onwards, and was particularly popular in North America.

BALLER
A small tool used for making spherical shapes of fruit.

BRANDRETH
An early implement for holding baking pots just off the direct heat of the fire. They were later replaced by trivets (see below).

BAKELITE
An early form of plastic invented by L.H. Baekeland in 1909 and used to make a variety of domestic objects.

BEATER
The North American term for a rotary whisk.

CAUDLE CUP
In England the term generally refers to a bulbous side cup which was used for caudle, a type of spicy, usually milk-based, porridge.

CRIMPER
A tool that adds attractive decorated edges to pastry.

EARTHENWARE
A type of pottery that is made with porous clay and that requires a sealant glaze (unlike stoneware or porcelain).

ENAMEL
Coloured glass, applied to metal, ceramic or glass in paste form and then fired for decorative effect. Enamelled kitchenware includes bread bins and other storage containers, saucepans and pie plates.

FLOUR DREDGER
A canister-shaped container that holds flour. It dredges (sprinkles) the flour when it is shaken upside down.

FLOUR SIFTER
A cup with a mesh across the base. Flour is sifted (in order to remove the course particles) by turning a handle which moves revolving blades through the flour. The flour then passes, sifted, through the mesh base.

FORCER
A cloth bag that was used to make meringues or decorative mounds of creamed potatoes in the 19th century. Forcers were gradually replaced in the early 20th century by syringe icing bags which have different sized nozzles.

GRANITEWARE
The North American term for enamelware.

GRIDDLE
A simple type of cookware, comprising a flat sheet of iron with a handle. Dating from Roman times, griddles were originally made from slate or sandstone.

IRONSTONE
A type of stoneware that was patented in 1813 by Charles James Mason, in which slag from iron furnaces is mixed into the clay, greatly toughening the ware.

JIGGER
A tool that adds attractive decorated edges to pastry.

LEAD GLAZE
A clear glaze generally composed of silicaeous sand, salt, soda and potash mixed with a lead component such as litharge (lead monoxide).

PIE FUNNEL
A pie funnel or cup, sometimes in the shape of a blackbird, is placed in the centre of a pie dish and pokes up through the pastry to support the pie and let out steam from the filling. In North America, all pie funnels and cups are known as pie birds, whatever shape they are.

PANCHEON
A deep, usually earthenware, bowl, that is traditionally used for the mixing and rising of yeast dough.

PARER
A tool for peeling apples.

PORRINGER
A double saucepan, mostly used for making custards, sauces and porridge.

PYREX
A type of glass that can withstand both rapid changes of temperature and attacks from chemicals.

RASP
A device which is used for scraping the burnt bottoms of loaves and also for making bread crumbs. .

REAMER
The North American term used to decribe any domed fruit juice squeezer. (See also squeezer below.)

REDWARE
A type of American clay pottery which turns red-brown when fired.

RASP
A device which is used for scraping the burnt bottoms of loaves and also for making bread crumbs.

RICER
A device for preparing mashed potatos, which turns it into rice-shaped grains.

SALT GLAZE
A thinly applied glaze used for covering stonewares. Salt is added to the hot kiln and fuses with the clay to create a glassy surface.

SLIP
A creamy mixture of clay and water, which is used to decorate pottery and also used for slip casting and sprigged wares.

SPURTLE
A traditional Scottish kitchen utensil used for stirring and mixing porridge.

SQUEEZER
The British term used to describe all fruit juicers. In North America the term is used for a juicer with hinged arms. (See also reamer above.)

STAINLESS STEEL
A highly practical type of steel developed in 1910, which was first used for making cookware and other kitchen utensils in the 1920s.

STONEWARE
A type of ceramic that is impervious to liquids. It is fired at a higher temperature than earthenware.

TAMIS
Another term for a cook's sieve, available with either a hair, wire or nylon base. Also known as a drum sieve.

TERRACOTTA
Lightly-fired red earthenware, usually unglazed.

TRIMMER
A type of tool that can make attractive decorated edges to pastry.

TRIVET
A stand on which to rest a pan, cooking pot or kettle.

USEFUL ADDRESSES

WHERE TO BUY

The following shops and dealers offer a range of collectable kitchenware and related items. Markets and fairs are good hunting grounds too.

PETER ADAMS
Jones Arcade
Portobello Road
London W11
(Saturdays only)

BAZAR
82 Goldbourne Road
London W10

BELOW STAIRS
103 High Street
Hungerford
Berkshire

CHRISTINA BISHOP
KITCHENWARE
CONSULTANT
c/o The Crazy Clothes
Connection
134 Lancaster Road
London W11

JANET CLARKE
ANTIQUARIAN BOOKS
3 Woodside Cottages
Freshford
Bath
Avon
(By appointment only)

THE DINING ROOM SHOP
52–64 White Hart Lane
Barnes
London SW13

THE DOG HOUSE
309 Bloxwich Road
Walsall
West Midlands

ANN LINGARD
Rope Walk Antiques
Rye
East Sussex

JUDY GREENWOOD
ANTIQUES
765 Fulham Road
London SW6

GREY & CO.
DESIGN CONSULTANTS
Fyning Copse
Rogate
Petersfield
Hampshire

LUNN ANTIQUES
86 New Kings Road
Chelsea
London SW6

MAGPIE ANTIQUES
152 Wandsworth
Bridge Road
Fulham
London SW6

ANNIE MARCHANT
26 Cornwallis Road
London N19
(by appointment only)

GUIMON MOUNTER
Baskers Farm
Dulford
Devon

NO 7 ANTIQUES
7 Nantwich Road
Woore
Shropshire

THE POT BOARD
30 King Street
Carmarthen

KEITH SKEEL ANTIQUES
7–9 Elliot Place
London N1

ROBERT YOUNG ANTIQUES
68 Battersea Bridge Road
London SW11

WHERE TO VISIT

AUDLEY END HOUSE
Saffron Walden
Essex

AYDON CASTLE
Corbridge
Northumberland

BADDESLEY CLINTON
Solihull
Nr. Warwick
Warwickshire

BARRINGTON COURT
Barrington
Somerset

BLICKLING HALL
Blickling
Nr. Great Yarmouth
Norfolk

BOLSOVER CASTLE
Bolsover
Chesterfield
Derbyshire

BOSCOBEL HOUSE
Wolverhampton
Shropshire

BRADLEY MANOR
Newton Abbot
Devon

BUCKLAND ABBEY
Yelverton
Nr. Exeter
Devon

BRODSWORTH HALL
Brodsworth
South Yorkshire

CALKE ABBEY
Ticknall
Derby
Derbyshire

CANONS ASHBY
Canons Ashby
Daventry
Northamptonshire

CARLYLE'S HOUSE
24 Cheyne Row
Chelsea
London SW3

CARLISLE CASTLE
Carlisle
Cumbria

CASTLE COOLE
Enniskillen
Co. Fermanagh
Northern Ireland

CASTLE DROGO
Drewsteignton
Nr. Exeter
Devon

CASTLE WARD
Strangford
Downpatrick
Co. Down
Northern Ireland

CHARLECOTE PARK
Charlecote
Warwick
Warwickshire

CLANDON PARK
West Clandon
Guildford
Surrey

CLEVEDON COURT
Tickenham Road
Clevedon
Nr. Yatton
Avon

COMPTON CASTLE
Marldon
Paignton
Devon

COTEHELE
St. Dominick
Nr. Saltash
Cornwall

CRAGSIDE HOUSE
Rothbury
Northumberland

DUNHAM MASSEY
Altrincham
Cheshire

ERDDIG
Nr.Wrexham
Clwyd

FLORENCE COURT
Enniskillen
Co. Fermanagh
Northern Ireland

GREAT CHALFIELD
MANOR
Nr. Melksham
Wiltshire

GAINSBOROUGH
OLD HALL
Gainsborough
Lincolnshire

GEFFRYE MUSEUM
Kingsland Road
London E2

HAM HOUSE
Richmond
Surrey

HAMPTON COURT PALACE
Hampton
Middlesex

HARDWICK HALL
Doe Lea
Chesterfield
Derbyshire

KENWOOD HOUSE
Hampstead
London NW1

LANHYRDROCK
Bodmin
Cornwall

LINDISFARNE CASTLE
Berwick-upon-Tweed
Northumberland

NO 1 ROYAL CRESCENT
Bath
Avon

ROYAL PAVILION
Brighton
East Sussex

PENDENNIS CASTLE
Falmouth
Cornwall

PORTLAND CASTLE
Portland
Dorset

SALTRAM
Plympton
Devon

SHAW'S CORNER
Ayot St. Lawrence
Nr. Welwyn
Hertfordshire

SHUGBOROUGH ESTATE
Milford
Nr. Stafford
Staffordshire

SPEKE HALL
The Walk
Liverpool
Merseyside

TATTON PARK
Knutsford
Cheshire

TEMPLE MANOR
Rochester
Kent

TOWNEND
Troutbeck
Windemere
Cumbria

UPPARK
Petersfield
West Sussex

WALLINGTON
Cambo
Morpeth
Northumberland

BIBLIOGRAPHY

SOCIAL HISTORY & REFERENCE

Adburgham, Alison, *Shops and Shopping 1800-1914*, Barrie & Jenkins, 1989

Adburgham, Alison, *Yesterday's Shopping: Army & Navy Stores Mail Order Catalogue 1907*, David & Charles, 1969

Atkinson, Frank, *Pictures from the Past: Northern Life*, Collins and Brown, 1991

Beck, Doreen, *The Book of Bottle Collecting*, Hamlyn, 1973

Bowers, Brian, *Electricity in Britain*, The Electricity Council, 1981

Mrs. Beeton's Book of Household Management, Isabella Beeton, Ward Lock, 1861

Briggs, Asa, *A Social History of England*, Weidenfeld & Nicholson, 1983

Black, Maggie, *Food and Cooking in Nineteenth Century Britain*, English Heritage, 1985

Brydson, John, *Plastic*, Her Majesty's Stationery Office, 1991

Byers, Anthony, *The Willing Servants, A History Of Electricity In The Home*, The Electricity Council, 1981

Coates, Doris, *Tuppeny Rice and Treacle: Cottage Housekeeping 1900-1920*, David & Charles, 1975

Corbishley, Gill, *Appetite for Change, Food and Cooking in Twentieth Century Britain*, English Heritage, 1993

Corbishley, Gill, *Ration Book Recipes: Some Food Facts 1939-1954*, English Heritage, 1990

Davies, Jennifer, *The Victorian Kitchen*, BBC Books, 1989

Davidson, Caroline, *A Woman's Work Is Never Done*, Chatto & Windus, 1982

Emmerson, Robin, *Table Settings*, Shire Publications, 1991

Forty, Adrian, *Objects of Desire: Design and Society 1750-1980*, Thames and Hudson, 1986

Holley, Erica, *Food*, Dryad Press, 1985

Garth, Margaret and Wrench, Stanley, *Home Management*, Daily Express Publications, 1934

Griffith, David, *Decorative Printed Tins*, Studio Vista, 1979

Household Encyclopedia, Harmsworth, 1923

Kitchen, Penny, *Women's Institute Magazines 1919-1959*, Ebury Press, 1990

Opie, Robert, *The Art of the Label*, Simon and Schuster, 1987

Plimmer, Violet G., *Food Values in Wartime*, Longmans & Green, 1941

Powers, Alan, *Shopfronts*, Chatto & Windus, 1989

Russell, Loris S., *Handy Things To Have Around The House*, McGraw-Hill Ryerson Ltd., 1979

KITCHENWARE

Allen, Col. Bob, *A Guide to Collecting Cookbooks*, Collector Books, 1990

Aresty Esther B., *The Delectable Past*, Simon & Schuster, 1964

Barile, Mary, *Cookbooks Worth Collecting*, Wallace-Homestead Book Company, 1993

Barlow, Ronald, S., *A Price Guide to Victorian Houseware, Hardware, and Kitchenware*, Windmill Publishing Co., 1992

Campbell, Susan, *The Cook's Companion*, Macmillan, 1980

Campbell Franklin, Linda, *300 Years of Housekeeping Collectibles*, Books of Americana, 1992

Campbell Franklin, Linda, *300 Years Of Kitchen Collectibles Book One*, Books Americana, 1991, (*Book Two*, 1993)

Card, Dever A., *The American Hearth: Colonial and Post-Colonial Cooking Tools*, Broome County Historical Society, undated

Cowan, Ruth Schwarz, *More Work for Mother*, Basic Books, 1983

Divone, Judene, *Chocolate Molds, A History & Encyclopedia*, Oakton Hills Publications

Eveleigh, David, *Old Cooking Utensils*, Shire Publications, 1986

Florence, Gene, *Kitchen Glassware of the Depression Years*, Collector Books, 1990

Gould, Mary Earle, *Early American Woodenware and other Kitchen Utensils*, Pond Ekberg Company, 1948

Greenstein, Lou, *A La Carte: A Tour of Dining History*, PBC International Inc., 1993

Harris, Gerturde, *Pots & Pans*, 101 Productions, 1971

Ingram, Arthur, *Dairying Bygones*, Shire Publications, 1977

Lasansky, Jeannette, *Willow, Oak & Rye: Basket Traditions in Pennsylvania*, Union County Oral Traditions Projects, 1978

Lindenberger, Jan, *Black Memorabilia for the Kitchen: A Handbook and Price Guide*, Schiffer, 1992

McCallister, Lisa and Michel, John L., *Yellow Ware, an Identification and Value Guide*, Collector Books, 1993

McConnell, Kevin, *Redware, America's Folk Pottery*, Schiffer, 1988

McNerney, Kathryn, *Kitchen Antiques 1790–1940*, Collector Books, 1991

Plante, Ellen M., *Kitchen Collectibles, An Illustrated Price Guide*, Wallace-Homestead Book Company, 1991

Roering, Fred and Joyce, *The Encyclopedia of Cookie Jars*, Collector Books, 1993

Stoneback, Diana, *Kitchen Collectibles, The Essential Buyer's Guide*, Wallace-Homestead Book Company, 1994

Thornton, Don, *Beat This: The Eggbeater Chronicles*, Offbeat Books, 1994

Weaver, William Ways, *American Eats*, Harper & Row, 1989

INDEX

Page numbers in **bold** refer to main entries.

ACKNOWLEDGMENTS

The publishers would like to thank the following people for supplying pictures for use in this book or for allowing their pieces to be photographed.

jkt front CB; **jkt back** AM; **1** CB; **2** JM; **4** CB; **5** CB; **6** AM; **7** AB; **8** JMO; **10** JMO; **11** P; **12** JM; **13** CB; **14 t** CB, **b** B; **15 t** B, **cr** CB, **b**(x2) CB; **16** (x2) CB; **16** (x2) CB; **17 cl, br** CB, **cr** CR, **bl** AM; **18** (x2) CB; **19 br** CB&B, **c, br** CB; **20 bl** JF, **br**CB; **21 t** CB, **br** CB, **cl** AM, **bl** AM; **22 tl** CS,**bl** CB; **23 l** CB, **r** AM, **br** CB; **24** AM; **25** (x4) CB; **26** (x3) CB; **27** (x3) CB; **28** (x2) CB; **29** (x3) CB; **30 tl** KL; **31** (x3) CB; **32** JM; **33** AM; **34** (x2) CB; **35 tr, bl** CB, **cl** AM, **br** RK; **36 tl** CB, **bl** CB, **br** AM; **37** (x3) CB; **38** (x2) CB; **39** (x2) CB; **40** (x2)CB; **41 tr** RW, **bl** CB; **42** JM; **43** AM; **44 t** CB&CS, **c** CDW; **45 tl** CS, **cr** CS, **b** CB; **46** (x2) AM; **47 tr** Am, **bl** CB, **br** CB; **48** (x2) CB; **49** (x3) CB; **50** JM; **51** RK;

52 (x2) CDW; **53** (x3) CB; **54** (x2) CB; **55 t** CB, **cl** CDW, **cr** CB, **b** CB; **56** CB; **57 t** CB, **cr**AM, **bl, br** CB; **58 t** CB, **l** CB, **b** AM; **59** (x3) CB; **60** (x2) CB; **61** (x3) CB; **62** (x2) CB; **63** (x2) CB; **64** (x2) CB, **bl** AP; **65 tr** CDW, **cl, br** CB; **66** (x3) CB; **67** (x4) CB; **68** (x4) CB; **69** (x3) CB; **70 tl** CB, **bl** CB, **br** CDW; **71 tr** CB, **bl** CDW, **br**CB; **72** (x2) CB; **73 tl, c, br** CB, **bl** CB&AS; **74 t**CB, **b** CB&CDW; **75 t** CB, **l** AM, **c** AM, **b** CB; **76 tl, tr, br** CB, **bl** CB&CDW; **77 tl, cr** CB, **tr, bl** CDW; **78** JM; **79** CB; **80 r** CB, **l** CB&CDW; **81 tl** CB, **bl** CB, **cl** AM, **cr** AM, **b** CB&CDW; **82** (x2) CB; **83** (x3) CB, **br** KL; **84** (x3) CB; **85** (x2) CB, **tr** KL; **86 t** CB, **b** CB&CDW; **87 tl, c, b** CB, **tr** CS; **88** (x3) CB; **89** (x4) CB; **90 t** AM, **b** CB; **91** (x3) CB; **92** JM; **93** AM; **94** CB; **95 t**CB&CDW, **r** CB, **l** CB; **96** (x3) AM; **97** (x3) AM; **98** CB; **99 t, r** CB, **bl** AP, **br** CS; **100** (x3) CB; **101** (x3) CB; **102 t** CB, **c** AM, **b** CB; **103** (x5) CB; **104** (x2) CB&CDW; **105** (x3) CB; **106** CB;

107 (x5) CB; **108 t** CB, **b** AM; **109 t, r, br** CB, **bl** CS; **110** JM; **111** CDW; **112** (x2) CB; **113** (x3) CB; **114** (x2) CB; **115 tl, tr** CB, **cl** CL, **cr** CB&CDW; **116 tl** CB&CL, **br** CB; **117** (x2) CB; **118** (x2) CB; **119** (x3) CB; **120** (x2) CB, **br** KL; **121** (x3) CB; **122** (x3) CB; **123** (x2) CB; **124** JM; **125** CB; **126** CBx2; **127** (x3) CB; **128** (x2) CB; **129** (x3) CB **130 t** JC, **b** HB; **131 t** JC, **c** BFC, **bl** BFC, **br** BFC; **134** (x3) DC; **135** (x2) DC

Key

b bottom
c centre
l left
r right
t top

B Bazar, 82 Goldbourne Road, W10
BFC Books for Cooks,
CB Christina Bishop
HB Harrington Brothers,
CDW Clarissa Dickson-Wright
DC David Cheadle
JC Janet Clarke
JF Josephine Fairley
RK Rosie Kindersley

CL Caroline Lindell
KL Kevin Lordan
AM Annie Marchant,
JM James Merrell
JMO James Mortimer, by kind permission of Johnny Grey
AP Andrew Peffers
P Phillips
CR Christine Rodgers
CS Craig Sams
RW Robin Weir

The Author would like to thank the following people for their help and encouragement: Pollie Bishop, Jane Conway-Gordon, Mel Cotton, Stephen Grey, Annie Marchant, Henrietta Palmer, Norman Coe, Lorraine Tabony, Peter Adams and all my customers past and present.

Q509A90C

MILLER'S ORDER FORM

TITLE	PRICE	QTY	TOTAL (£)
ANTIQUES			
1857326164 Miller's Antiques Price Guide 1996	£19.99		
1857326091 Miller's Picture Price Guide 1996	£19.99		
1857325427 Miller's Collectables Price Guide 1995/6	£16.99		
1857326849 Miller's Pine & Country Furniture Buyer's Guide	£16.99		
1857326857 Miller's Art Nouveau & Art Deco Buyer's Guide	£16.99		
1857326571 Miller's Collecting Furniture: The Facts At Your Fingertips	£9.99PB		
1857321790 Miller's Antiques & Collectables: The Facts At Your Fingertips	£8.99PB		
1857320018 Miller's Understanding Antiques	£14.99PB		
0855336897 Miller's Pocket Antiques Fact File	£6.99		
1857322703 Miller's Rock & Pop Memorabilia	£14.99		
1857323505 Miller's Golf Memorabilia	£14.99		
1857321677 Miller's Royal Memorabilia	£14.99		
1857325842 Miller's How To Make Money Out Of Antiques	£4.99		
INTERIORS			
185732398X Period Kitchens	£16.99		
1857320433 Period Details	£14.99		
1857323017 Period Style	£14.99		
1857320980 Victorian Style	£25.00		
0855337664 Country Style	£25.00		
	Total		
	P&P (see note)		
	Payment due		

Postage & Packing Charges
Please add £1.50 for all orders under £10.00.
Postage and packing is FREE for orders of £10.00 and over to UK, NI, BFPO.
For delivery outside the UK, please add £3.00 per order towards carriage.

All books are hardback unless otherwise shown. The prices were correct at the time of going to press, but Miller's reserve the right to increase prices at short notice.

How to order
Simply use the order form and return it to us with your credit card details or a cheque/postal order made payable to Reed Book Services or telephone the credit card hotline on 01933 414000.

Method of Payment
1. I attach a cheque or postal order to the value of £..............
2. Please debit my ACCESS/VISA/AMEX/DINERS CARD (please delete) by the amount shown.

NAME (block letters)...
ADDRESS...
....**POSTCODE**.................................

Card Number

Expiry Date

Signature...

Send your completed form to: **Miller's Club, Reed Book Services Limited, PO Box 5, Rushden, Northants NN10 6YX**
All titles are subject to availability. Orders are normally despatched within 5 days, but please allow up to 28 days for delivery.
If you do not wish you name to be used by other carefully selected organisations for promotional purposes, please tick this box.
Registered office: Michelin House, 81 Fulham Road, London SW3 6RB. Reg. in England no. 1974080.